FIRST AID

FIRST ON THE SCENE

ACTIVITY
BOOK

FIRST EDITION 2000

St. John Ambulance

First Edition – 2000
First Printing – January 2001
Fourth Printing – April 2002
Fifth Printing – December 2002
Sixth Printing – August 2003

St. John Ambulance
1900 City Park Drive
Ottawa, Ontario
K1J 1A3

Canadian Cataloguing in Publication Data

Main entry under title:

    First aid : first on the scene: activity book

ISBN 1-894070-20-8

    1. First aid in illness and injury. 2. CPR (First aid). 3. First aid in illness
and injury—Problems, exercises, etc. 4. CPR (First aid)—Problems, exercises, etc.
I. St. John Ambulance.

RC86.8.F592 2000   616.02'52   C00-901629-5

Printed in Canada
Stock No. 6500-01

CONTENTS

STUDENT INFORMATION

St. John Ambulance courses are nationally recognized standardized programmes. They are based on performance objectives and well defined training standards which are contained in the Instructor's Guide for these courses.

This **self-instruction activity book** is part of a sequenced training programme, consisting of videos, instructor-led practical and activity book exercises.

Certification requirements

The training standards specify the minimum requirements for certification. Courses may be expanded, if necessary, to include additional material required to meet local needs.

To receive a certificate you must:

◆ attend the instructional sessions

◆ obtain a satisfactory pass on the practical exercises, and

◆ obtain a minimum mark of 70% on each section of the written examination

Your first aid certificate is valid for three years from the date the course was successfully completed. Your CPR certificate has no expiry date, however annual certification is recommended.

Note: First aid skills deteriorate very quickly unless they are practised regularly. Recertification every three years in first aid and annual retraining in CPR is recommended.

The Manual

First on the Scene, The Complete Guide to First Aid and CPR is the reference manual for this course. You may purchase the manual from your instructor, the local branch of St. John Ambulance, or any book store. You may use the manual:

◆ as supplementary reading during the course

◆ as reference material after the course

USE OF THE ACTIVITY BOOK

Before starting your activity book exercises, you should have completed the Course Registration Form contained at the back of this activity book and have handed it to your instructor.

Welcome to the activity book exercises.

This self-instruction book will help you to learn the first aid theory for the course and will prepare you for the final written examination. Your instructor will tell you which

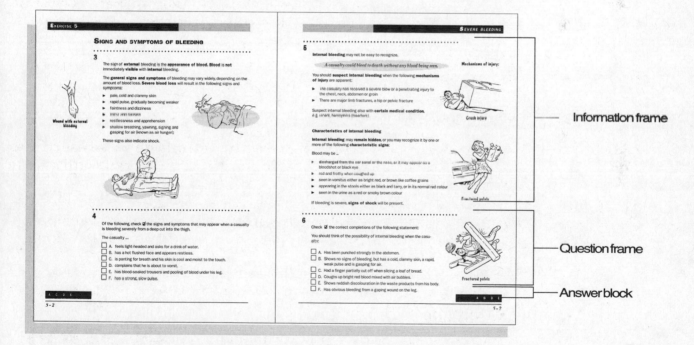

exercises to complete and when to do them.
Each exercise consists of **teaching units** called **frames**.

Each frame is numbered and contains either:

◆   **information** for you to read, or

◆   **questions** for you to answer

The **correct answer** to each question appears in the **answer block** located at the bottom of the page.

How to do the activity book exercises

1. Tear off the **cursor** attached to the back cover.

2. Use the cursor to cover the answer block until you have marked your answers to the question.

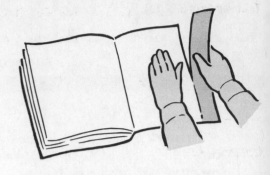

3. To **check** your answers, **slide the cursor to the side** as far as the end of the answer block. This will **reveal the correct** answer(s) in the answer block.

4. If your answer is wrong, read the question again, draw a line through your wrong answer and write in the correct one.

5. If you do not know the answer to a question, look at the answer frame, mark the correct answer in the appropriate space and read the question again.

There are several types of questions used in this activity book to reinforce your learning. Four examples are given below:

Multiple choice type:

Check ☑ the correct completion to the statement below.

The aim of first aid for a minor, open wound is to:

☐ A. Prevent itching.

☐ B. Send the casualty to medical help.

☐ C. Control bleeding and prevent infection.

☐ D. Check the area around the wound.

Note: Multiple choice questions may have more than one right answer.

c

True or false type:

Mark each of the following statements as true **(T)** or false **(F)**:

☐ A. Spurting blood is more difficult to stop than flowing blood.

☐ B. Bleeding always looks the same, no matter where it comes from.

A.T B.F

Order type:

Number the following first aid actions in the order you should perform them:

☐ A. Send for medical help.

☐ B. Assess responsiveness.

A.2 B.1

Match type:

Match each situation with the appropriate safety measure.

Situations	Safety measures
☐ A. A girl gulps down a soft drink while chewing on her hamburger.	1. Avoid other activities when you are eating.
☐ B. A man eats a sandwich while trying to steer his car.	2. Don't eat and drink at the same time.

A.2 B.1

Instructor-led exercises:

The Instructor-led exercises will give you the opportunity to discuss and develop key ideas with the help of your instructor. To fill in the blanks properly, your instructor will give you the appropriate information. Should you do your activity book exercises at home, the answers to the instructor-led exercises are contained in Addendum B.

Instruotor-lcd Exercise

A. Good air exchange	B. Poor air exchange	C. No air exchange
A1. The person _____ speak.	B1. The person _____ speak.	C1. The person _____ speak.
A2. The facial colour is _____ .	B2. The facial colour is _____ .	C2. The facial colour is _____ .
A1. can	B1. cannot	C1. cannot
A2. reddish	B2. bluish	C2. bluish

EXERCISE 1

EMERGENCY SCENE MANAGEMENT

Introduction to first aid

1

What is first aid?

First aid symbol

First aid is the emergency help given to an injured or suddenly ill person using readily available materials.

The objectives of first aid are to:

◆ preserve life
◆ prevent the injury or illness from becoming worse
◆ promote recovery

Who is a first aider?

A first aider is someone who takes charge of an emergency scene and gives first aid.

First aider arriving at the scene with a first aid kit

Why is first aid important?

◆ You may recognize an emergency early and call for help quickly
◆ You may keep someone alive by giving first aid
◆ Wounds have a better chance of healing if you give prompt and appropriate first aid.

2

What can you do as a first aider?

You can help a person in need. Whenever you help a person in an emergency situation, you should abide by the **Principles of the Good Samaritan**, and:

◆ **act in good faith** and volunteer your help

◆ **tell the person you are a first aider**

◆ **get permission** (consent) to give first aid before touching the casualty. Use your common sense and consider the age and the condition of the casualty

◆ **ask** the parent or guardian for permission if the person is an infant or young child

◆ **have implied consent**. If the person does not **respond** to you, you can give first aid. Implied consent exists because the casualty is unconscious

◆ **use reasonable skill and care** according to your level of knowledge and skills. Unless limited by a provincial statute, the care that is given to a person will be measured against what a reasonable person with similar knowledge and skills would do

◆ **do not abandon (leave) the person** once your offer of help has been accepted. Stay until:

  ◆ You hand the person over to medical help

  ◆ You hand the person over to another first aider

  ◆ The person no longer wants your help

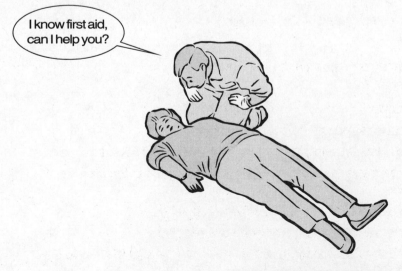

I know first aid, can I help you?

Identify yourself as a first aider

3

What is medical help?

Medical help is the treatment given by, or under the supervision of, a medical doctor at an emergency scene, while transporting a casualty, or at a medical facility.

What is a casualty?

A person who is injured or who suddenly becomes ill is called a casualty.

Doctor arriving on scene

Age guidelines for a casualty

For first aid and CPR techniques, a casualty is considered to be:

◆ **an adult** – eight years of age and over

◆ **a child** – from one to eight years of age

◆ **an infant** – under one year of age

Adult

Child

Infant

Ambulance arriving

Use these guidelines with **common sense** in choosing the appropriate first aid and CPR techniques. Consider the size of each casualty when making your decision.

Casualty with first aider

4

Mark each of the following statements as true **(T)** or false **(F)**.

☐ A. The Good Samaritan Laws will protect you no matter what

☐ B. If the person is unconscious you cannot touch him or her

☐ C. First aid is considered "medical help", if you have taken a first aid course

☐ D. An ambulance attendant gives "medical help" because he works under the supervision of a doctor

☐ E. A choking person who is unable to breathe is called a casualty

☐ F. The term infant describes a baby who is less than one year old

☐ G. A very small nine year old should be treated as an adult when you give first aid

A.F B.F C.F D.T E.T F.T G.F

Universal precautions in first aid

. . . .

5

Some people are afraid to give first aid. They think they might catch a disease from the casualty, but people are most likely to be helping family and friends. The risk of a **serious** infection being transmitted is small but there are several types of disease you should be aware of when providing first aid.

Diseases caused by viruses and bacteria can be spread through the blood (bloodborne pathogens) or in the air through coughing or sneezing (airborne pathogens). There are many different types of diseases spread by either of these routes but a select few are of interest to first aiders.

Bloodborne Infections: There are 3 types of bloodborne disease that first aiders should be particularly aware of:

1. Human immunodeficiency virus (HIV). This virus is responsible for AIDs which affects the body's immune system and its ability to fight other diseases. Currently no vaccine exists to protect people from this virus and the best defense remains adequate protection to help prevent infection.

2. Hepatitis B. Hepatitis is a viral disease of the liver that can cause severe liver damage or liver cancer. There are 3 common forms of hepatitis -Type A, Type B and Type C depending on the type of virus causing the disease. Health care workers are at high risk for contacting this disease as are others involved in first response such as police officers, firefighters etc. Some people who have hepatitis B have no symptoms but can still have the virus in their blood and are therefore contagious. Fortunately a vaccine does exist that will prevent hepatitis B from occuring and the vaccine is usually made available to high risk individuals.

3. Hepatitis C. Hepatitis C causes much the same liver damage as hepatitis B but there is currently no vaccine available to prevent this disease

Airborne Infections. A number of diseases can be spread through the air usually by a person inhaling droplets when an infected person coughs or sneezes. The common cold is a good example but more serious diseases such as tuberculosis are also spread in this fashion.

One of the best ways first aiders can protect themselves from the chance of catching a disease is by using "Universal Precautions" as explained on the following page.

Universal precautions in first aid

5

Use the following **universal precautions** to minimize risk and give first aid safely. Disagreeable factors (vomitus, incontinence, blood, odours) are very common, but can also be avoided with **barrier devices.**

◆ **Wash your hands** with soap and running water immediately after any contact with a casualty

◆ **Wear vinyl or latex gloves** whenever you might be in touch with the casualty's blood, body fluids, open wounds or sores

◆ **Handle** sharp objects with extra care

◆ **Minimize** mouth-to-mouth contact during artificial respiration by using **a mask** or **a face shield** designed to prevent disease transmission

A face mask or face shield should:

◆ have a **one-way valve**

◆ be **disposable** or have a disposable valve

◆ be stored in an **easily accessible** place

Follow the manufacturer's instructions on how to use, care for and dispose of a mask and shield properly.

Face shields with one-way valves

Pocket Mask

Face Shield

Be prepared. Ensure your first aid kit includes disposable gloves and a face mask/shield

If you have to clean up a blood spill use personal protection such as gloves. Wipe up the spill using paper towels or other absorbent material. After you have cleaned up the area cover it with a bleach solution (1/4 cup bleach (15mL) to 1 gallon(4 litres) of water) and let stand for at least 20 minutes . Cleaning materials contaminated with blood or other body fluids should be discarded in appropriate containers.

Clothing that has been stained with blood or vomitus should be thoroughly washed in a washing machine in hot water.

How to remove gloves

6

Gloves that have been used are contaminated and may spread infection. Take them off without touching the outside. Follow the steps below:

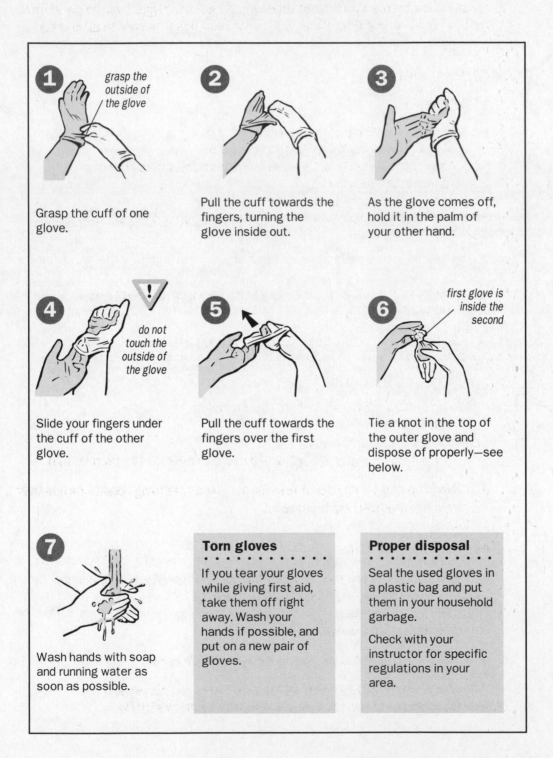

1 *grasp the outside of the glove*

Grasp the cuff of one glove.

2 Pull the cuff towards the fingers, turning the glove inside out.

3 As the glove comes off, hold it in the palm of your other hand.

4 *do not touch the outside of the glove*

Slide your fingers under the cuff of the other glove.

5 Pull the cuff towards the fingers over the first glove.

6 *first glove is inside the second*

Tie a knot in the top of the outer glove and dispose of properly—see below.

7 Wash hands with soap and running water as soon as possible.

Torn gloves

If you tear your gloves while giving first aid, take them off right away. Wash your hands if possible, and put on a new pair of gloves.

Proper disposal

Seal the used gloves in a plastic bag and put them in your household garbage.

Check with your instructor for specific regulations in your area.

Principles of emergency scene management (ESM)

7

Scene survey

Emergency scene management (ESM) is the sequence of actions you should follow at the scene of an emergency to ensure that safe and appropriate first aid is given. Following the steps of emergency scene management will help you make **rapid and accurate decisions** to give the best possible care to a casualty.

ESM has four steps:

Scene Survey

Primary survey

◆ Where you take charge of the situation and:
- assess hazards and make the area safe
- assess history, determine the number of casualties and the mechanism of injury
- assess responsiveness

◆ You should call or send for medical help if any of these are a problem

Primary Survey

◆ Where you examine the casualty for life threatening conditions:
- Airway
- Breathing
- Circulation

Secondary Survey

Secondary survey

◆ Where you establish and record the casualty's:
- personal medical history
- vital signs baseline and
- look for secondary injuries with a detailed head-to-toe examination

◆ This step may be omitted if first aid for life-threatening conditions has been given and medical help is close by

Ongoing Casualty Care

Ongoing casualty care

◆ Where you keep the casualty comfortable and monitor him to ensure:
- an open Airway in an unconscious casualty
- effective Breathing
- and treat for Circulation (Shock)

◆ Give an oral report when you handover to medical help

Emergency scene management starts with the scene survey and ends when you have handed over the casualty to medical help.

Scene survey

8

The order of steps in the scene survey may change, but in most cases, you will do them in this order:

Take charge of the situation. If head/spinal injuries are suspected, tell casualty not to move

Call out to attract bystanders

Assess hazards at the scene and make the area safe for yourself and others, put on protective gloves if available

Determine the history:
- the number of casualties,
- what happened and the mechanism of injury

Important information when you are assessing the mechanism of injury includes:
- the type of force
- the height of a fall
- the speed of a vehicle involved
- the location on the body

The greater the force, height or speed, the more likely it is that injuries will be life-threatening. **Suspect head/spinal injuries** if the casualty has received a great deal of force, especially to the head

Scene survey

Identify yourself as a first aider:

- offer to help
- obtain consent from a conscious casualty
- an unconscious casualty has given implied consent

8 Scene Survey - cont'd

If head/spinal injuries are suspected, do not move the casualty. Provide and maintain manual support for the head and neck

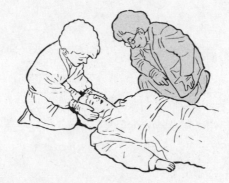

Assess the casualty's responsiveness.

If there are **hazards**, obvious **serious injuries,** or if the casualty is not **responsive,** send or go for **medical help**

9

Mark each of the following statements as true **(T)** or false **(F)**.

 A. When approaching an emergency scene, the first thing you should do is take the lead and try to get someone to help

☐ B. At a car crash site, you give first aid without worrying about further dangers to yourself and the casualty

☐ C. To give appropriate first aid, you should check how many people are hurt and how badly

☐ D. Before you touch an injured person, you should introduce yourself and ask if you can help

☐ E. If you think that a casualty's neck has been hurt, tell him not to move. Steady his head and neck with your hands or show a bystander how to do this

A.T B.F C.T D.T E.T

10

To help you decide what first aid to give to a casualty, you should find out as much as possible about the casualty's injury or illness. You need three kinds of information:

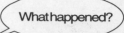

What happened?

- ◆ history
- ◆ signs and
- ◆ symptoms

History

- ◆ **Ask** the conscious casualty "what happened?"
- ◆ **Ask** bystanders "what happened?"
- ◆ **Observe** the scene, what is the mechanism of injury?

What do I see, hear, feel, smell?

Signs

Signs are conditions of the casualty **you can see, hear, feel or smell.**

- ◆ **Observe** the casualty
- ◆ **Examine** for indications of injury or illness

Symptoms

Symptoms are **things the casualty feels** and may be able to describe.

- ◆ **Ask** the conscious casualty how she feels
- ◆ **Listen** to what the casualty says

How do you feel?

11

Identify the information of each statement below as either history, sign or symptom by writing the appropriate number in the boxes provided.

History ☐1 Sign ☐2 Symptom ☐3

- ☐ A. A casualty tells you he feels cold
- ☐ B. There is blood soaking through the shirt on a casualty's arm
- ☐ C. A casualty's skin is cold and clammy to the touch
- ☐ D. A man tells you that he slipped on a patch of ice
- ☐ E. A young boy says he feels sick
- ☐ F. You see an empty bottle of sleeping pills near an unconscious person

A.3 B.2 C.2 D.1 E.3 F.1

Primary survey

12

The primary survey is the first step in assessing the casualty for life-threatening conditions and giving life-saving first aid.

In the primary survey you check for the **priorities of first aid**. These are:

A. **Airway** – to ensure a clear airway

B. **Breathing** – to ensure effective breathing

C. **Circulation** – to ensure effective circulation

Even if there is more than one casualty, you should perform a primary survey on each casualty. Give life-saving first aid only.

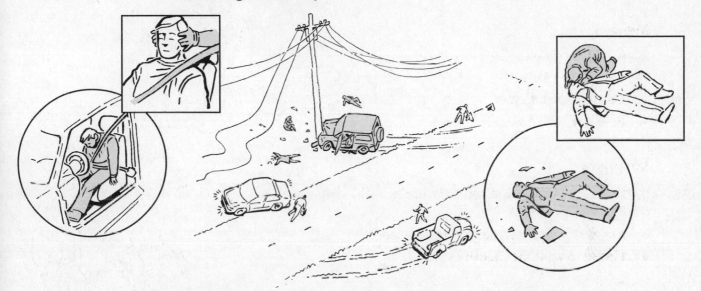

13

From the following statements, check ☑ all correct endings to the following two statements.

The purpose of the primary survey is to:

☐ A. Find all injuries

☐ B. Find the conditions posing an immediate danger to life

☐ C. Give complete treatment to all injuries

Immediate threats to life include the following conditions:

☐ D. A blocked airway

☐ E. Severe bleeding inside the body

☐ F. A broken arm

☐ G. Stopped breathing

B D E G

Steps of the primary survey

14

The sequential steps of the primary survey should be performed in **the position found**, unless it is impossible to do so.

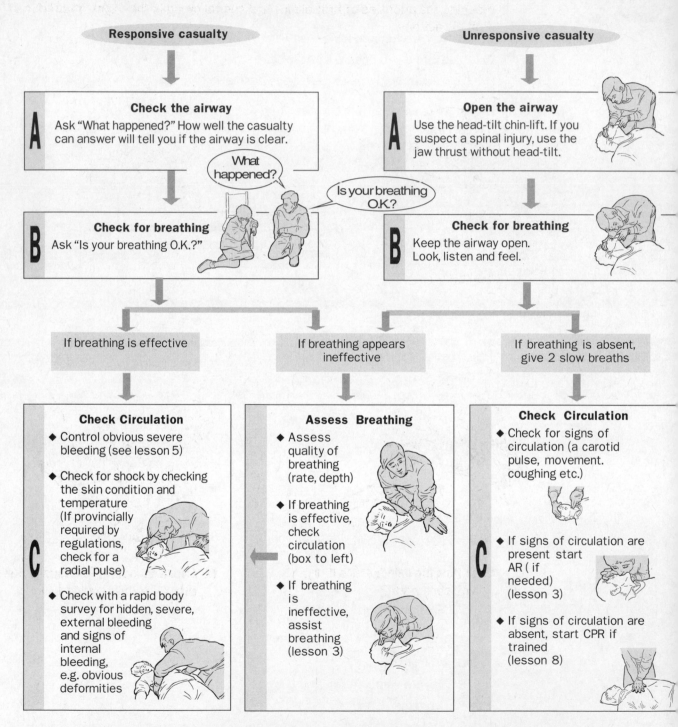

Responsive casualty

Unresponsive casualty

A **Check the airway**
Ask "What happened?" How well the casualty can answer will tell you if the airway is clear.

What happened?

A **Open the airway**
Use the head-tilt chin-lift. If you suspect a spinal injury, use the jaw thrust without head-tilt.

B **Check for breathing**
Ask "Is your breathing O.K.?"

Is your breathing O.K.?

B **Check for breathing**
Keep the airway open. Look, listen and feel.

If breathing is effective

If breathing appears ineffective

If breathing is absent, give 2 slow breaths

C **Check Circulation**
◆ Control obvious severe bleeding (see lesson 5)

◆ Check for shock by checking the skin condition and temperature (If provincially required by regulations, check for a radial pulse)

◆ Check with a rapid body survey for hidden, severe, external bleeding and signs of internal bleeding, e.g. obvious deformities

Assess Breathing
◆ Assess quality of breathing (rate, depth)

◆ If breathing is effective, check circulation (box to left)

◆ If breathing is ineffective, assist breathing (lesson 3)

C **Check Circulation**
◆ Check for signs of circulation (a carotid pulse, movement. coughing etc.)

◆ If signs of circulation are present start AR (if needed) (lesson 3)

◆ If signs of circulation are absent, start CPR if trained (lesson 8)

When you check the ABC's, give first aid as soon as you find any life-threatening condition.
If you find any deformities, manually steady and support the injured part until medical help takes over.

15

You have finished the scene survey. The mechanism of injury does not lead you to suspect a spinal injury. You know that the casualty is unresponsive. This means you have consent to help. You have to do the primary survey to find out if the casualty has any life-threatening injuries.

Keeping the priorities of first aid in mind, the following is the **right sequence** of first aid actions.

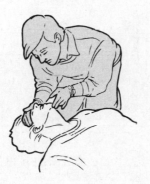

A.   Open the airway.

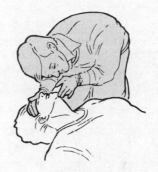

B.   Check breathing.

C.   Check how the skin feels. Is it dry, wet, cool, warm?

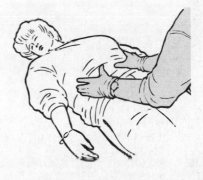

D.   Check quickly if the casualty has other life-threatening injuries.

Ongoing casualty care

16

Following immediate first aid, you must **maintain the casualty in the best possible condition until hand over to medical help**.

- Instruct a bystander to maintain manual support of head and neck, if head/spinal injuries are suspected
- Continue to steady and support any injuries manually, if needed
- Give first aid for shock
  - ❖ reassure the casualty often
  - ❖ loosen tight clothing
  - ❖ place the casualty in the best position for her injury or illness (lesson 2)
  - ❖ cover the casualty to preserve body heat
- Monitor the casualty's condition (ABC's) and note any changes
- Give nothing by mouth
- Record the casualty's condition, any changes that may occur and the first aid given
- Protect the casualty's personal belongings
- Do not leave the casualty until medical help takes over
- Hand over to medical help and report on the incident, the casualty's condition and the first aid given

Shock position

Supporting head and neck

Recovery position

17

An ambulance is expected soon.

Which of the actions listed below should you take to care for a conscious casualty following immediate first aid? Check off ☑ your choices.

- ☐ A. Place a blanket under and over the casualty to maintain body temperature
- ☐ B. Check skin temperature and condition frequently
- ☐ C. Provide hand support to injured body parts
- ☐ D. Leave the casualty alone without further checking
- ☐ E. Report to medical personnel on the casualty's condition and the help given
- ☐ F. Make sure that the casualty doesn't lose any valuables

A B C E F

SHOCK, UNCONSCIOUSNESS AND FAINTING

1

Shock is a condition of **inadequate circulation** to the body tissues. It results when the brain and other vital organs are deprived of oxygen. The development of shock can **be gradual or rapid.**

Shock may be present with any injury and illness.

Shock can be life threatening and needs to be recognized and cared for immediately.

Common causes of severe shock	
Cause of shock	**How it affects the circulation**
◆ breathing problems (ineffective or absent breathing)	not enough oxygen in the blood to supply the vital organs
◆ severe bleeding, external or internal, including major fractures	not enough blood in circulation to supply all vital organs
◆ severe burns	loss of fluids, reducing amount of blood to fill the blood vessels
◆ spinal cord injuries	nervous system can't control the size of blood vessels and blood pools away from vital organs
◆ heart attack	heart is not strong enough to pump blood properly
◆ medical emergencies, e.g. diabetes, allergies, poisoning	these conditions may affect breathing, heart and nerve function

Signs and symptoms of shock

2

The **signs** and **symptoms** of shock may not be obvious immediately, but any of the following may appear as shock progresses.

You may see:

- restlessness
- decreased consciousness
- pale skin at first, later bluish grey
- bluish/purple colour to lips, tongue, earlobes and fingernails*
- cold, clammy skin
- profuse sweating
- vomiting
- shallow, irregular breathing; could be rapid and gasping for air
- a weak, rapid pulse (in later stages the radial pulse may be absent)

* **Note:** If the casualty has dark skin, the inside of the lips, the mouth, the tongue and the nail beds will be blue; the skin around the nose and mouth greyish.

The casualty may tell you of:

- feelings of anxiety and doom
- being confused and dizzy
- extreme thirst
- nausea
- faintness
- pain

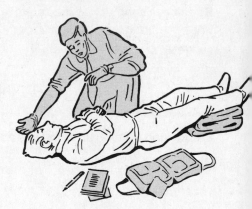

Check skin condition

3

From the choices below, check ☑ the correct completion for the following statement. Write the appropriate choice number in the boxes provided:

When a casualty is in shock, usually the . . .

		Choice 1	OR	Choice 2
☐	A. skin is	white		reddish
☐	B. skin is	dry		moist
☐	C. skin is	warm		cold
☐	D. breathing is	fast		slow
☐	E. pulse is	fast		slow
☐	F. casualty feels	calm		uneasy
☐	G. casualty feels	thirsty		hungry

A.1 B.2 C.2 D.1 E.1 F.2 G.1

First aid for shock

4

To prevent shock from becoming worse:

◆ **give prompt and effective first aid for any injury or illness**

◆ reassure the casualty often

◆ loosen tight clothing at neck, chest and waist

◆ place the casualty into the best position for the condition

◆ cover the casualty to preserve body heat

◆ place a blanket under the casualty, if available. Ensure movement does not aggravate injuries

◆ give nothing by mouth

◆ moisten lips only if the casualty complains of thirst

◆ monitor the casualty's condition (ABC's) and note any changes

◆ continue ongoing casualty care until hand over to medical help

Shock position
feet and legs raised
about 30 cm (12 inches)

Conscious casualty

Covered casualty in shock position

5

A conscious casualty is bleeding from a large slash on his forearm. His skin is cold and moist. His lips and earlobes appear bluish. Of the following, check ☑ the first aid actions you should take to prevent the casualty's condition from becoming worse.

☐ A. Give immediate first aid for the wound

☐ B. Place the casualty into the recovery position

☐ C. Place covers under and over the casualty to keep him warm

☐ D. Give the casualty water to drink since he is complaining of severe thirst

☐ E. Rub the casualty's limbs vigorously to improve his circulation

☐ F. Avoid causing the casualty more discomfort

A C F

Positioning of a casualty in shock

6

The **position** you use for a casualty **depends on the casualty's condition.** Always consider the casualty's comfort when choosing a position.

◆ To prevent further injury, support a casualty with suspected head/spinal injuries in the:

Position found

◆ To ease breathing, place a casualty with breathing difficulty, e.g. heart attack, asthma, into the:

Semisitting position

◆ To maintain an open airway, place the unresponsive casualty into the:

Recovery position

◆ To increase blood flow to the vital organs, place the conscious casualty into the:

Shock position

First aid for shock—review

7

Your friend is working alone in a wood workshop. The chain saw slips and causes a large slash in your friend's lower arm. The cut is bleeding profusely and your friend is pale and sweating as you arrive.

The sequence of actions you would follow at this emergency scene to give appropriate first aid and slow down the progress of shock is:

1. Survey the scene.

2. Check the airway by asking: "Where do you hurt?"

3. Check breathing by asking: "Is your breathing O.K.?"

4. Expose the wound and control severe bleeding.

5. Check the skin condition and temperature; and perform a rapid body survey.

6. Give ongoing casualty care.

Unconsciousness

● ●

8

When you assess a casualty and find her unresponsive, you should immediately:

◆ send, or go for medical help

If the casualty remains unresponsive, she is considered to be unconscious.

Unconsciousness indicates a serious medical situation. Many injuries and illnesses are complicated by the loss of consciousness, e.g. head injuries, breathing emergencies, heart attack, poisoning, shock and fainting.

Unconsciousness is a *breathing emergency*.

If the unconscious casualty is lying on his back, the airway may become blocked by the tongue falling to the back of the throat, or by fluids draining into the airway. Maintaining effective breathing is the *first priority*.

◆ Look, listen and feel to determine if the casualty is breathing
◆ **Recheck breathing** frequently
◆ If the casualty stops breathing, give artificial respiration immediately

First aid for an *unconscious* casualty (when medical help is on the way)

◆ Perform a primary survey
◆ Give first aid for any life-threatening conditions
◆ Loosen restrictive clothing
◆ Place the casualty into the recovery position, if injuries permit
◆ Give ongoing casualty care until hand over to medical help

Any change in the casualty's condition should be observed and noted, and described to medical personnel when the casualty is handed over.

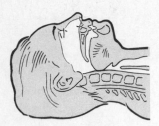

Tongue blocking
the airway

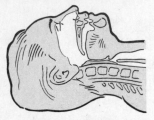

Fluids blocking
the airway

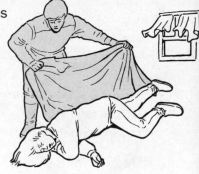

Recovery position

● ●

9

A woman collapses in the shopping mall. When you call out to her and tap her on the shoulders, you determine that she is unresponsive (unconscious). Order the following actions according to your priorities by placing the appropriate number in the squares provided:

☐ A. Ask a bystander to telephone for an ambulance
☐ B. Apply first aid for life-threatening conditions
☐ C. Loosen the casualty's collar and belt
☐ D. Perform a primary survey
☐ E. Place the casualty in the recovery position, if injuries permit

A.1 B.3 C.4 D.2 E.5

Fainting

10

Fainting is a brief loss of consciousness caused by a **temporary shortage of oxygen to the brain.**

Fainting may be caused by:

◆ fatigue, hunger or lack of fresh air

◆ fear and anxiety

◆ long periods of standing or sitting

◆ severe pain, injury or illness

The following may warn you that a person is about to faint:

◆ you may observe paleness and sweating

◆ the casualty may complain of feeling sick and dizzy

 First aid for the person who feels faint

Act quickly (you may be able to prevent her from fainting):

◆ lay the person down with legs raised about 30 cm (12 in) (the shock position)

◆ ensure a supply of fresh air

◆ loosen tight clothing around the neck, chest and waist

If you cannot lay the person down:

◆ have the person sit with her head and shoulders lowered

 First aid for the person who has fainted

A person who has fainted is temporarily unconscious. The first aid is the same as for the person who is unconscious (see opposite page).

When the casualty regains consciousness:

◆ make her comfortable

◆ keep her lying down for 10 to 15 minutes

Sitting position

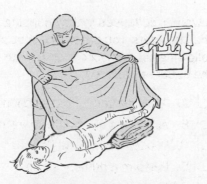

Shock position

Notes

∙∙

ARTIFICIAL RESPIRATION–ADULT

Introduction to breathing emergencies

1

We must breathe to live!

Breathing is the movement of air in and out of the lungs.

Air is taken in and out of the lungs by **the respiratory system** which has three main parts:

◆ the airway
◆ the lungs and
◆ the diaphragm

Air reaches our lungs through the **airway**.

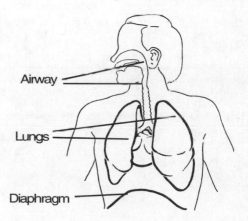

Respiration is the process of exchange of oxygen (O_2) and carbon dioxide (CO_2) in the body.

◆ The air we breathe in contains **21% oxygen,** which is important to life

◆ The air we breathe out contains **5% carbon dioxide**, a waste product of the body, but still contains **16% oxygen**

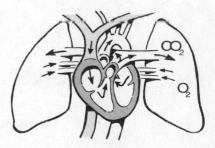

Gas Exchange

Causes of breathing emergencies

2

The causes of breathing emergencies can be classified into **three major groups:**

1 there is not enough oxygen in the air

- ◆ suffocation
- ◆ near-drowning

Be particulary careful of confined spaces such as storage tanks, silos etc. Special training and equipment is required to rescue casualties trapped in confined spaces. Wait for professional help before providing first aid.

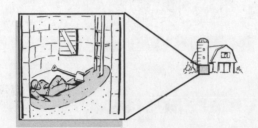 

2 the heart and lungs are not working properly

- ◆ heart attack
- ◆ head/spinal injuries
- ◆ electric shock
- ◆ open chest wound
- ◆ poisoning/drug overdose

3 the airway is blocked—the person is choking

- ◆ airway obstruction
- ◆ allergic reactions, e.g. asthma

Signs of breathing emergencies

3

When breathing **stops** or is **ineffective**, the body is deprived of oxygen. This is called a breathing emergency.

After **4 minutes** without oxygen, brain damage may result.

You must act immediately to restore or assist breathing!

Be alert for signs of breathing emergencies:

Breathing has **stopped**, when . . .

◆ the chest does not rise and fall
◆ air movement cannot be heard or felt

Ineffective breathing is generally characterized by . . .

◆ very slow and shallow breaths, 10 or less per minute
◆ very fast and shallow breaths, about 30 or more per minute
◆ laboured and noisy breathing, gasping for air
◆ sweaty skin
◆ fatigue
◆ a bluish colour to the skin
◆ decreased level of consciousness

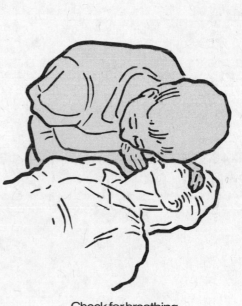

Check for breathing

4

From the following statements, check ☑ the signs which may indicate a breathing emergency:

☐ A. The chest expands and relaxes with ease
☐ B. Rapid, irregular chest movement
☐ C. No chest movement when you watch for breathing
☐ D. Regular and quiet breaths
☐ E. A casualty's lips and earlobes show blue discolouration
☐ F. A great effort needed to breathe, making the casualty very tired

B C E F

Effective breathing

5

Effective breathing usually is . . .

◆ without pain or effort
◆ easy and quiet
◆ with even steady rhythm

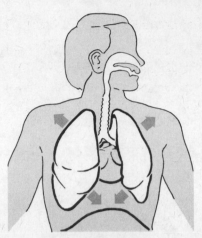

To check the **effectiveness** of the casualty's breathing, you assess the . . .

◆ breathing rate
◆ breathing depth and quality
◆ skin colour

Breathing in—
lungs inflate

Breathing rate

◆ Is the number of breaths in one minute
◆ The average breathing rate for a healthy adult at rest is in the range of
10 to 20 breaths per minute

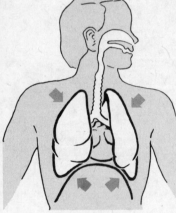

Breathing out—
lungs deflate

6

Mark each statement below as true **(T)** or false **(F)**:

☐ A. A person having 14 breaths a minute fits within the normal range of breathing

☐ B. Breathing in and breathing out should be smooth and painless

☐ C. A casualty's breathing is adequate, when you observe deep, sucking breaths

☐ D. If you suspect that a casualty's breathing is ineffective, count the number of breaths per minute and check the skin colour

☐ E. You should immediately try to breathe for a person who shows no signs of air moving in or out of the lungs

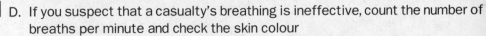
A.T B.T C.F D.T E.T

First aid for breathing emergencies

7

When breathing stops, a person requires **immediate first aid**.

◆ You must get oxygen into the casualty's lungs

◆ The oxygen content of the air you breathe out is 16% by volume, **enough to sustain** the life of a non-breathing person. The best way to do this is by blowing into the casualty's mouth. This is called **mouth-to-mouth artificial respiration (AR)**

Mouth-to-mouth AR

Mouth-to-mouth with face mask

Blowing into the casualty's nose is another method of AR, the **mouth-to-nose method of AR**.

◆ Use the mouth-to-nose method when . . .

❖ the mouth cannot be opened

❖ the casualty has injuries about the mouth or jaw

❖ your mouth cannot fully cover the casualty's mouth

8

From the listing below, check ☑ the correct statements relating to first aid for a non-breathing casualty.

☐ A. You can keep a person alive by blowing into her mouth or nose

☐ B. The mouth-to-mouth method of AR is the best way you can get air into the casualty's lungs

☐ C. If a casualty has a broken chin, use the mouth-to-mouth method of AR

☐ D. For a casualty who has wounds around the lips, your choice of AR should be the mouth-to-nose method

A B D

3-5

Mouth-to-nose method of AR

∙ ∙

9

The basic techniques for the mouth-to-nose method are the same as for the mouth-to-mouth, **except that you breathe through the casualty's nose**.

The mouth-to-mouth method is modified for the mouth-to-nose method by the following techniques:

- ◆ **tilt** the head back using the head-tilt chin-lift
- ◆ **close** the casualty's mouth with your thumb
- ◆ **cover** the casualty's nose with your mouth to give ventilations
- ◆ **give a ventilation and watch** the chest rise
- ◆ **open** the casualty's mouth between breaths and remove your mouth from the casualty's nose to let the air out
- ◆ **look**, **listen** and **feel** for air movement

Mouth-to-mask AR allows mouth-to-nose ventilations, but some barrier devices (face shield with one way valve) do not allow a mouth-to-nose seal.

Mouth-to-nose

Mouth-to-nose with face mask

Assisted breathing

. . . .

10

You may have to assist a casualty to breathe if he has severe breathing difficulties.

The **responsive** casualty may resist your efforts to assist breathing.

◆ **Reassure** the casualty and **explain** what you are trying to do and why it is needed

◆ Do not attempt to assist breathing if the casualty remains uncooperative

The **unresponsive** casualty with ineffective breathing . . .

◆ is in urgent need of your assistance

Mouth-to-mouth with shield
(head-tilt chin-lift)

How to provide assisted breathing

The technique for assisted breathing is the same as for mouth-to-mouth AR, except for the timing of the ventilations.

If the breathing rate is below 10 breaths per minute . . .

◆ match the casualty's inhalations. Give additional ventilations between the casualty's own breaths to a combined total of 1 breath every 5 seconds

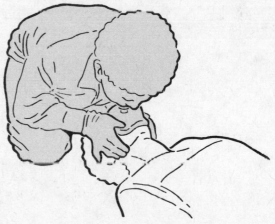

If the breathing rate is greater than 30 breaths per minute . . .

◆ assist every second breath to slow the casualty's breathing rate. This will result in more effective breathing

Mouth-to-mouth with face mask
(jaw-thrust)

Gastric distension and vomiting during AR

11

Common complications of AR are gastric distension and **vomiting,** usually caused by **increased air in the stomach**. This happens when . . .

◆ the airway is not completely open
◆ ventilations are given **too quickly** and with **too much force** causing air to enter the stomach. This prevents effective ventilation

Gastric distension

To reduce the risk of gastric distension:

◆ ensure an open airway
◆ give slow breaths
◆ use **just** enough air to make the chest rise

Vomiting

If vomiting occurs during AR:

◆ turn the casualty to the side with her head turned down
◆ wipe the mouth clear of vomitus
◆ reposition the casualty on her back
◆ reassess breathing and circulation
◆ resume ventilations if necessary

Artificial respiration—review

· ·

12

You witness a near-drowning on a beach with a few bystanders standing around the casualty. It wasn't a diving incident and there is no indication of head/spinal injuries. You take charge and begin emergency scene management.

The first aid actions for this casualty **in the order you should perform them** are:

1. Assess responsiveness.

2. Send a bystander to get medical help.

3. Open the airway.

4. Check for breathing.

5. Give two slow breaths.

6. Check for signs of circulation.

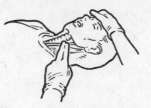

7. Continue giving one breath every five seconds.

8. Check for breathing and signs of circulation after 1 minute.

Notes

· ·

EXERCISE 4
....

CHOKING–ADULT

discolouration of lips,
earlobes and fingernails

universal sign
of choking

☞ ## Signs of choking and first aid
....

1

A person chokes when the airway is partly or completely blocked and airflow is reduced or cut off. A choking person may die if first aid is not given **immediately**.

A person's airway can be either: **partially** or **completely** blocked.

A **partially** blocked airway results in either:

◆ **good air exchange**

◆ **poor air exchange**

With a **completely** blocked airway, there is:

◆ **no air exchange**

....

2 **Instructor-led Exercise 4**

A. Good air exchange	B. Poor air exchange	C. No air exchange
A1. The person _____ speak.	B1. The person _____ speak.	C1. The person _____ speak.
A2. Coughing and gagging are _____	B2. Coughing and gagging are _____	C2. Coughing and gagging are _____
A3. You may hear _____ _____ when trying to breathe.	B3. You may hear _____ _____ when trying to breathe.	C3. There will be _____; the person _____ breathe.
A4. The facial colour is _____	B4. The facial colour is _____	C4. The facial colour is _____
A5. Stand by and _____ _____	B5. Start _____ for choking.	C5. Start _____ for choking.

Answers: Addendum B

Causes and prevention of choking

3

Choking is a life-threatening **breathing emergency**. A choking person may die if first aid is not given **immediately.**

Common causes of choking are:

◆ food or some other object stuck in the throat

◆ the tongue of an unconscious casualty falling to the back of the throat

◆ blood or vomit collects in the throat of an unconscious casualty

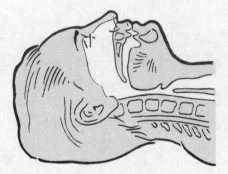

Clear airway

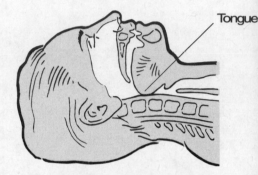

Tongue

Blocked airway by tongue

4

Check ☑ the correct answers from either choice 1 or choice 2 to complete the following statements.

Choice 1   OR   **Choice 2**

When a casualty is choking and has poor or no air exchange . . .

A. ☐ the air passages are clear   ☐ the air passages are blocked

B. ☐ there is little or no air getting to the lungs   ☐ air flows freely into and out of the lungs

C. ☐ his life is in danger   ☐ his life is not in danger

When a casualty is unconscious . . .

D. ☐ his air passages open wider   ☐ his tongue may block the air passages

A.2 B.1 C.1 D.2

5

Choking may be caused by:

◆ trying to swallow large pieces of food

◆ eating and drinking while doing something else

◆ drinking too much alcohol before or during a meal

◆ gulping drinks with food in your mouth

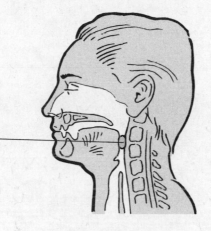

Food chunk

Airway blocked by food chunk

Avoid choking by taking these precautions:

◆ chew food well before swallowing

◆ avoid talking and laughing while chewing food

◆ drink alcohol in moderation before and during meals

◆ avoid other physical activities while eating

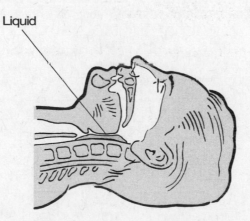

Liquid

Airway partially blocked by liquid

Self-administered first aid for choking

6

Abdominal thrusts

When you are alone and choke and **you cannot speak, breathe or cough,** you can help yourself.

◆ Try to call for medical help or attract attention

Using your hands:

◆ place a fist above your navel

◆ grasp the fist with the other hand

◆ press inward and upward forcefully. Make each thrust distinct, with the intent to dislodge the obstruction

◆ repeat thrusts until the obstruction is relieved

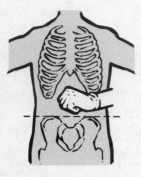

Abdominal thrusts

Using furniture:

◆ position your abdominal area, slightly above the hips, along the counter, table edge or the back of a chair

◆ press forcefully into the edge to apply pressure. Make each thrust distinct, with the intent to dislodge the obstruction

◆ repeat thrusts until the obstruction is relieved

7

Chest thrusts

When you are in the **late stages of pregnancy** or if you are **very obese,** abdominal thrusts cannot be applied effectively.

◆　Try to call for medical help or to attract attention

The following procedure creates a pressure similar to a chest thrust performed by a first aider:

◆　make a fist and place it thumb side down in the middle of your chest
◆　with your head turned to the side, fall against a wall hard enough to produce a chest thrust
◆　make each thrust distinct, with the intent to clear the obstruction
◆　repeat this procedure until the obstruction is relieved

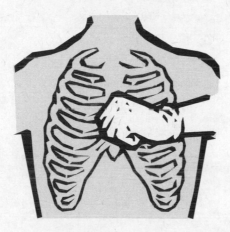

Chest thrusts

8

When you give first aid for choking, which of the following persons would require chest thrusts?

Check ☑ your choices.

☐　A.　An average sized woman who is conscious
☐　B.　A young man who is extremely overweight
☐　C.　A young woman in her last month of pregnancy
☐　D.　A very tall and muscular athlete

First aid for choking—review

9

The following questions are based on the videos, your practical exercises and this activity book exercise.

A choking person clutches her throat, is red in the face and is coughing forcefully and loudly.

From the first aid procedures shown below, check ☑ the appropriate action you should take.

☐ A. Landmark for abdominal thrusts.

☐ B. Stand by and encourage coughing.

☐ C. Give up to five chest thrusts.

☐ D. Give up to five abdominal thrusts.

10

A choking person is conscious and has great difficulty breathing. Her lips are bluish and she is unable to answer your question, "Are you choking?"

From the first aid procedures shown below, check ☑ the one action you should take immediately.

☐ A. Use a hooked finger sweep in the casualty's mouth to remove the obstruction.

☐ B. Send for medical help immediately.

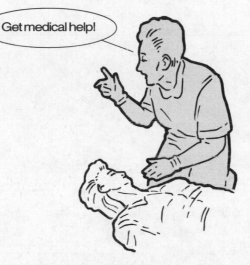

Get medical help!

☐ C. Encourage the casualty to cough up the obstruction.

☐ D. Give abdominal thrusts until the obstruction is relieved or the person becomes unconscious.

D

11

A conscious choking casualty becomes unconscious. Here the first aid actions for this casualty **in the order you should do them**.

1. Ease her to the floor and call or go for medical help.

2. Look for obstruction. Remove with a hooked finger if seen.

3. Open the airway and check for breathing for up to 10 seconds

4. Try to ventilate, if air does not go in, reposition the airway and try again

5. Landmark - Give 15 chest compressions

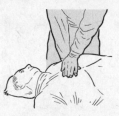

6. Look for obstruction again

7. Try to ventilate, if necessary reposition the airway and try again, if necessary continue compressions

8. Continue compressions and attempts to ventilate until airway is clear

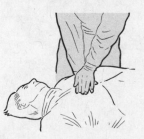

Ongoing casualty care until hand over

12

When a choking person's airway has been cleared and you have completed the primary survey, if ...

◆ the casualty **remains conscious:**
  ❖ monitor breathing and circulation frequently
  ❖ stay with the casualty until breathing is well established and skin colour has returned to normal
  ❖ urge the casualty to see a medical doctor

◆ the casualty **regains consciousness:**
  ❖ monitor breathing and circulation frequently
  ❖ give first aid for shock
  ❖ stay with the casualty until medical help takes over
  ❖ urge the casualty to see a medical doctor

◆ the casualty **remains unconscious:**
  ❖ monitor breathing and circulation frequently and assist breathing if necessary
  ❖ place the casualty into the recovery position
  ❖ give first aid for shock
  ❖ stay with the casualty until medical help takes over

Note: Choking manoeuvres can cause internal damage.

C A U T I O N

Breathing problems, and other signs of choking may be caused by swelling in the airway due to an allergic reaction to food or a bee sting, an infection or injury. Do not waste time trying to relieve this obstruction. Get medical help immediately.

13

Check ☑ the correct completions to the following statement. When an airway obstruction has been removed by abdominal or chest thrusts, and normal breathing has been restored, the casualty should:

☐ A. Require no medical help.
☐ B. Be observed closely to ensure complete recovery.
☐ C. Be placed into the recovery position if not fully conscious.
☐ D. Be seen by a doctor to check for possible injuries.

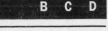
B C D

Notes

· ·

SEVERE BLEEDING

Wounds

1

A **wound is any break in** the continuity of **the soft tissues** of the body.

A wound usually **results in bleeding.** Depending on the location of the wound, it may be either . . .

◆ **external bleeding:** blood escapes from the surface wound and can be seen, or

◆ **internal bleeding:** blood escapes from tissues inside the body and cannot be seen directly

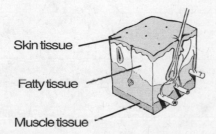

Skin tissue

Fatty tissue

Muscle tissue

Break in the continuity
of the soft tissues

Depending on the blood vessels that are damaged, bleeding can be either:

◆ **arterial bleeding:** blood is bright red and spurts with each heart beat from the damaged artery. Arterial bleeding is serious and often hard to control.

◆ **venous bleeding:** blood is dark red and flows steadily. It will stop more readily when being controlled.

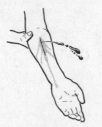

Arterial bleeding

Venous bleeding

Signs and symptoms of bleeding

2

The sign of **external** bleeding is the **appearance of blood. Blood** is **not** immediately **visible** with **internal** bleeding.

General signs and symptoms of bleeding may vary widely, depending on the amount of blood loss. **Severe blood loss** will result in the following signs and symptoms:

◆ pale, cold and clammy skin

◆ rapid pulse, gradually becoming weaker

◆ faintness and dizziness

◆ thirst and nausea

◆ restlessness and apprehension

◆ shallow breathing, yawning, sighing and gasping for air (known as air hunger)

These signs indicate **shock**.

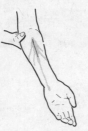

Wound with external bleeding

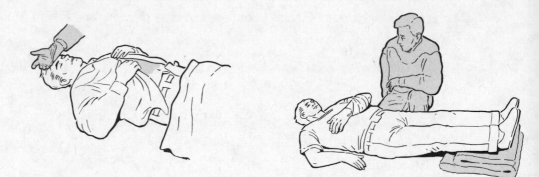

3

Of the following, check ☑ the signs and symptoms that may appear when a casualty is bleeding severely from a deep cut into the thigh.

The casualty . . .

☐ A. feels light-headed and asks for a drink of water

☐ B. has a hot flushed face and appears restless

☐ C. is panting for breath and his skin is cool and moist to the touch

☐ D. complains that he is about to vomit

☐ E. has blood-soaked trousers and pooling of blood under his leg

☐ F. has a strong, slow pulse

4

Internal bleeding may not be easy to recognize.

A casualty can bleed to death without any blood being seen.

You should **suspect internal bleeding** when the following **mechanisms of injury** are apparent:

◆ the casualty has received a severe blow or a penetrating injury to the chest, neck, abdomen or groin

◆ there are major limb fractures or a hip or pelvic fracture

Suspect internal bleeding also with **certain medical conditions**, e.g. ulcers, hemophilia (bleeders).

Mechanisms of injury:

Crush injury

Fractured upper leg (femur)

Fractured pelvis

Characteristics of internal bleeding

Internal bleeding **may remain hidden**, or you may recognize it by one or more of the following **characteristic signs**:

Blood may be . . .

◆ discharged from the ear canal, the nose, or it may appear as a bloodshot or black eye

◆ red and frothy when coughed up

◆ seen in vomitus either as bright red, or brown like coffee grains

◆ appearing in the stools either as black and tarry, or in its normal red colour

◆ seen in the urine as a red or smoky brown colour

◆ your rapid body survey may reveal swelling, unusual firmness or rigidity

If bleeding is severe, **signs of shock** will develop.

First aid principles for severe external bleeding

5

Severe bleeding is an immediate threat to life.
You must act quickly!
If bleeding remains uncontrolled, shock and death may result

Direct pressure

Elevation

Control severe bleeding by:

◆ **Direct pressure** to the bleeding site

❖ Apply continuous pressure with your hand over a pad of dressings, or with the casualty's bare hand. You may have to bring the edges of the wound together before applying pressure if the wound is large and gaping

❖ Continue pressure by securing dressings with a firm bandage

❖ If dressings become blood soaked, do not remove them. Apply additional dressings and secure with fresh bandages

◆ **Elevation**

❖ If injuries permit, raise an injured limb above the level of the heart. This will help reduce blood flow to the wound

❖ Elevate an injured limb as much as the injury and the casualty's comfort will permit

◆ **Rest**

❖ Place the casualty at rest. The preferred position is lying with lower legs raised about 30 cm (12 inches) if injuries permit

Remember the colour of blood: **R -** Rest
                                          E - Elevation
                                          D - Direct pressure

Steady and **support** the injured part and give ongoing casualty care while awaiting medical help.

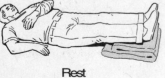

Rest

Impaired circulation

6

Some injuries and first aid procedures may result in reduced blood flow to the limbs:

◆ **injuries at, or close to, a joint** may pinch an artery

◆ **a bandage** that is too tight

◆ **injury to a major blood vessel**

Checking temperature before bandaging

To check for impaired circulation below the injury:

◆ **compare** the **temperature** and **colour** of the injured limb below the injury (fingers or toes) to the uninjured limb before and after bandaging

  ❖ any drop in temperature in the limb is probably caused by a reduced blood flow

Checking temperature after bandaging

◆ **perform a nailbed test**

  ❖ press on a fingernail or toenail until it turns white

  ❖ release pressure; note how long it takes for the normal colour to return

  ❖ if it returns quickly, blood flow is good

  ❖ if it remains white or regains colour slowly, blood flow is impaired

Nailbed test

To improve impaired circulation caused by too tight bandages, you should immediately:

◆ **loosen the bandages**; if bleeding starts again, re-tie the bandages

If circulation is still impaired:

◆ **obtain medical help** immediately, lack of adequate circulation will damage tissues

Untying bandage

Continue checking circulation until hand over to medical help.

Care of amputated tissue

7

In many cases amputated parts can be surgically reattached. Proper care of the amputated tissue, therefore, is very important. First control the bleeding, then:

For a completely amputated part, you should:

◆ wrap it in a clean, moist dressing, if possible; otherwise a clean dry dressing

◆ place it in a clean, watertight plastic bag and seal it

◆ place it into another bag with a cold pack or crushed ice to keep it cool

◆ label the bag with the casualty's name, date and the time it was wrapped

◆ take or send the part to medical help with the casualty

Care of a completely amputated part

For a partially amputated part, you should:

◆ keep it as near as possible to its normal position

◆ cover it with a moist dressing if possible; otherwise a dry dressing. Apply direct pressure on the wound to stop bleeding

◆ secure the dressings in place with a bandage

◆ obtain medical help as soon as possible

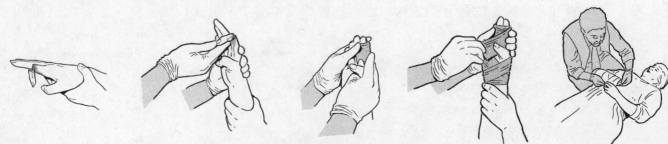

Care of a partially amputated part

First aid for internal bleeding

8

The most important thing, you as a first aider, can do is to:

◆ **recognize** the history and mechanism of injury that might cause internal bleeding

◆ **recognize** shock

◆ give **first aid for shock** to lessen its effects

◆ **obtain prompt medical help**

Shock position

While waiting for medical help, make the casualty as comfortable as possible.

◆ Place the **conscious** casualty at rest on his back with feet and legs elevated to about 30 cm (12 inches), if injuries permit

◆ Place the **unconscious**, breathing casualty into the recovery position

◆ Reassure the casualty

◆ Preserve body heat

◆ Give nothing by mouth

◆ Reassess airway, breathing and circulation

Recovery position

Recovery position covered

9

Which of the following would you do for a conscious casualty with suspected internal bleeding?

Check off ☑ your choices:

☐ A. Tell the casualty that he is bleeding badly inside his body

☐ B. Obtain medical help quickly

☐ C. Comfort the casualty with gentle encouragement

☐ D. Place a blanket under and over the casualty

☐ E. Allow the casualty to take sips of water

☐ F. If the condition allows, raise the casualty's lower legs on a folded coat

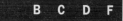
B C D F

Notes

· ·

CHILD RESUSCITATION

1

You will recall that for first aid and CPR techniques, a **child** is someone who is **between 1 and 8 years old**, according to the age group guidelines.

Cardiovascular disease is not very common in children. However, children can be taught how to prevent cardiovascular disease by learning about healthy food and good living habits.

It is more common for children to suffer **breathing emergencies** caused by disease or injury. Stopped breathing may lead to **cardiac arrest.**

- Breathing must be restored immediately

Some common **causes/mechanisms of injury** for stopped breathing in children are:

- injuries caused in car collisions
- a blocked airway (choking)
- suffocation
- electric shock
- strangulation

- near-drowning
- smoke inhalation and burns
- poisoning
- upper respiratory infection
- allergies

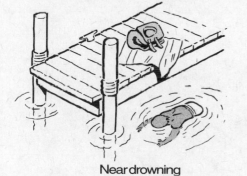

Near drowning

Suffocation

Anyone who cares for a child should know how to:

- **prevent** breathing emergencies, when possible
- **recognize** when breathing has stopped
- **act immediately** to restore breathing

Prevention of breathing emergencies

2

Small objects

The best way to protect children is to prevent emergencies from happening! Most emergencies in children can be prevented. **Injuries** are the biggest risk to children.

To help protect children, you should:

◆ use car seats and other child restraints that are properly installed

◆ teach children to be "street smart"
  ❖ how to use roads safely
  ❖ to wear bicycle helmets

Choking is the most common **breathing emergency** in children. It is usually caused when the airway is blocked by the tongue, food or small objects.

To prevent choking and other breathing emergencies, you should:

◆ place an unconscious, breathing child into the recovery position

◆ supervise young children when they are eating

◆ don't give young children nuts, popcorn, hard candies, etc.

◆ keep small objects such as marbles, toy parts and broken, uninflated balloons away from small children

◆ check toys and household objects for small detachable parts

◆ make sure children use their toys as recommended by the manufacturer

◆ enrol children in swimming lessons to help prevent near-drowning

◆ teach children about the dangers of electricity

◆ keep poisonous products, including medications, out of the reach of children

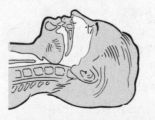

Dangerous food

Blocked airway by the tongue

Universal distress sign of choking

Artificial respiration

3

For a child, you should use the **mouth-to-mouth method** of **AR**. Use the same techniques as for an adult, with the following modifications:

- if you are alone go call for medical help, but carry the child with you if possible
    - remember, brain damage may result after as little as 4 minutes of stopped breathing
- give one breath **every 3 seconds**
- use slow breaths of air, **just** enough to make the chest rise, overventilation may cause gastric distension
- take **1 to 1.5 seconds** for each breath

Pulse and breathing rates vary according to the age of the person.

- The average **pulse rate** of a healthy child at rest is **80 to 100 beats** per minute
- The average, **breathing rate** of a healthy child at rest is about **20 to 30 breaths** per minute

Mouth-to-mouth AR

Check for signs of circulation

Carrying child

4

Mark each of the following statements as either true **(T)** or false **(F)**:

- ☐ A. Along with the age, the size of the child should be considered when giving artificial respiration
- ☐ B. A breathing rate of 20 breaths per minute is normal for a child
- ☐ C. The amount of air required to ventilate a small child is the same as for an adult
- ☐ D. When you are alone with a non-breathing child who has a pulse, it is important to call for an ambulance immediately
- ☐ E. The pulse and breathing rates of children and adults are the same

A.T   B.T   C.F   D.T   E.F

Signs of choking and first aid

5

When a child is choking, you may see the same signs as in an adult depending on the degree of obstruction. If he can cough effectively, encourage his efforts, stand by, ready to help. A very young child cannot show you, as clearly as an adult, that he has trouble breathing.

When a child has breathing difficulties caused by swelling of the tissues from an allergy or an infection, get medical help or take the child to the hospital immediately! Do not waste time trying to clear the airway.

Start first aid for choking immediately when you observe:

◆ the child choking on an object

◆ weak, ineffective coughing

◆ breathing becoming faster as the child tries to take in more air or it may become irregular, or may stop for short periods of time

◆ abnormal sounds such as wheezing or high-pitched noises

◆ a bluish tinge to the skin

◆ the child clutching his throat

◆ child cannot speak

Universal distress sign of choking

Differences in first aid for choking in children and adults:

◆ landmark and give abdominal thrusts for a conscious child from a position where the shoulders of the first aider and the child are at the same level, e.g. **kneeling position**

Remember, a child should always receive medical care following abdominal thrusts. This manoeuvre may cause internal damage.

6

Which of the following conditions might indicate that a child is choking on an object? Check ☑ the correct answers.

☐ A. A child is pale and sweating

☐ B. A child is gagging at the dinner table

☐ C. A playing child is eating peanuts and suddenly cannot make a sound

☐ D. A child has a high temperature and has great difficulty getting air

☐ E. A young child is staring wide-eyed with his hands on the front part of his neck

B C E

First aid for choking—review

7

You have already done a scene survey and assessed the child as unresponsive.
The first aid steps in the **order you should perform them**:

1. Send a bystander to get medical help.

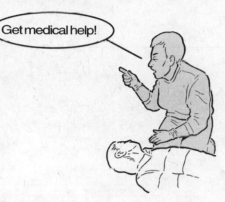

Get medical help!

2. Open the airway and check for breathing (not breathing).

3. Try to ventilate the lungs (chest does not rise) reposition the head and try again.

4. Begin compressions - landmark and give 5 chest compressions.

5. Open the airway and look for the obstruction (nothing visible).

6. Try to ventilate the lungs (chest does not rise) reposition the head and try again. Continue compressions.

Cardiopulmonary resuscitation (CPR)

8

CPR is two basic life-support skills put together—artificial respiration and artificial circulation.

CPR is used to circulate oxygenated blood to the tissues and maintain the life of a child when –

◆ breathing has stopped and
◆ circulation has stopped

Differences between adult and child CPR:

◆ use only the heel of one hand to give chest compressions
◆ use a ratio of 5:1 for chest compressions and ventilations
◆ compress the chest 2.5 to 3.8 cm (1 to 1.5 inches)

Checking for breathing

Checking for signs of circulation

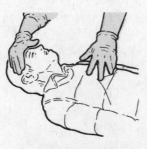

Landmarking

Chest compressions

Child CPR—review

9

You have already done the scene survey and found that the child is unresponsive. You have sent for medical help, the remaining first aid steps in **the order you should perform them are:**

1. Open the airway using the head-tilt chin-lift.

2. Check for breathing (not breathing).

3. Try to give two slow breaths (chest rises).

4. Check for signs of circulation, pulse, movement, etc. (no circulation)

5. Landmark for chest compressions.

6. Give cycles of 5 compressions and 1 ventilation for one minute.

7. Recheck for signs of circulation after one minute (not breathing, no pulse).

8. Continue cycles of 5 compressions and 1 ventilation.

Notes

· ·

EXERCISE 7

11minutes

INFANT RESUSCITATION

1

As you have learned before, the word **infant** describes a baby **up to 1 year** of age.

When an infant's **heart stops** beating it is usually not caused by a problem in the heart itself. Most often it is the result of a breathing emergency. After a short time without oxygen, the infant's heart will stop beating.

◆ You must give first aid for stopped breathing immediately

The most common **causes/mechanisms of injury** for breathing emergencies in an infant are:

◆ injuries
◆ choking on a foreign object
◆ smoke inhalation
◆ suffocation
◆ infection

◆ allergies
◆ strangulation
◆ electrocution
◆ near-drowning
◆ sudden infant death syndrome (SIDS)

Electrocution

Suffocation

Anyone who cares for an infant should know how to:

◆ **prevent** breathing emergencies, when possible
◆ **recognize** when breathing has stopped
◆ **act immediately** to restore breathing

How to prevent breathing emergencies

2

As with children, the best way to protect an infant, is to prevent a breathing emergency!

To protect an infant from injury you should:

◆ use car seats appropriate for the age of the infant and ensure they are properly installed

◆ use approved gates to close off stairways in your home

To protect an infant from breathing emergencies you should:

◆ check your child's pacifier. Make sure it is made in one piece

◆ check all toys for small parts that could break off

◆ always supervise infants when they are eating

◆ not leave a baby to feed himself with a propped-up bottle

◆ pick the baby up and hold him during feeding time

◆ keep plastic bags away from infants to prevent suffocation

◆ not leave an infant unattended on an adult waterbed

Small objects   Dangerous food

SIDS—Sudden Infant Death Syndrome

SIDS, also called crib death, is the unexplained death of an apparently healthy infant. The infant dies suddenly and unexpectedly, usually while sleeping. To help reduce the possible risk factors:

◆ put the baby to sleep on her back on a firm, flat surface

◆ do not use bumper pads, quilts, duvets or pillows in the crib

◆ keep the baby in a smoke-free environment

◆ do not overheat the baby

◆ breastfeed the baby, if possible

Parents should not feel that the death of their baby from SIDS is their fault. Research tells us how we may reduce the risks, but we cannot prevent all SIDS deaths. The actual cause of SIDS is still unknown.

The Canadian Foundation for the Study of Infant Deaths, Canadian Institute for Child Health, Canadian Pediatric Society, and Health Canada.

Artificial respiration

3

For infants and small delicate children you should use the **mouth-to-mouth-and-nose method** of artificial respiration.

To use the **mouth-to-mouth-and-nose method**, follow the same procedures as for the mouth-to-mouth method, with the following changes:

◆ if alone call for medical help, carry the infant with you, if possible, to the telephone.
   ◆ remember, brain damage may result after as little as 4 minutes of stopped breathing
◆ do not over extend the neck when opening the airway
◆ make a good seal with your mouth **over the mouth and nose** of the infant
◆ give one breath **every 3 seconds**
◆ use **slow breaths of air**, just enough to make the chest rise
◆ use the **brachial pulse** as one of the signs of circulation

Brachial pulse

4

Which of the following techniques are used when giving AR to an infant or very small child? Check ☑ your answers from the following two choices.

Choice 1	Choice 2
☐ A. Cover the mouth tightly.	☐ A. Cover the mouth and nose tightly.
☐ B. Blow into the mouth and nose with a strong force.	☐ B. Blow into the mouth and nose enough to make the chest move.
☐ C. Give ventilations at a faster rate than for an adult.	☐ C. Give ventilations at the same rate as for an adult.
☐ D. Take the pulse at the neck.	☐ D. Take the pulse on the inside of the upper arm.
☐ E. If you are by yourself, start AR before you call for an ambulance.	☐ E. If you are by yourself, call for an ambulance before you start AR.

A.2 B.2 C.1 D.2 E.2

The brachial pulse

. . . .

5

To **check if the heart is beating** and pumping blood to the vital organs, you must look for signs of circulation, including brachial pulse, movement, coughing, etc. when giving artificial respiration.

To check the **brachial pulse** on an infant:

◆ support the head to keep the airway open

◆ place the fingers on the inside of the upper arm and press lightly between the muscle and the bone to feel the pulse

◆ take no more than 10 seconds for the circulation check

◆ after about one minute of AR and every few minutes thereafter, recheck for breathing and signs of circulation for no more than 10 seconds

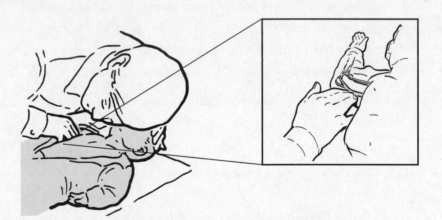

The brachial pulse

Be aware that the pulse can be difficult to find. Take no more than 10 seconds to assess circulation, if you are not sure do not delay, begin CPR.

An **infant's breathing and pulse rates** are faster than an adult's or a child's.

◆ The resting breathing rate of a healthy infant is about **30 to 50 breaths** per minute

◆ The resting pulse rate of a healthy infant is **100 to 140** beats per minute

Infant AR—review

6

Your neighbour calls for you to help. She cannot wake up her baby. The first aid procedures **in the correct order are:**

1. Call out "baby, baby" and tap the infant's feet.

2. Send the mother for medical help.

Get medical help!

3. Open the airway using the head-tilt chin-lift.

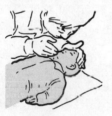

4. Look, listen and feel for breathing.

5. Cover the baby's mouth and nose and attempt to give 2 slow breaths.

6. Check for signs of circulation (there are signs of circulation).

7. Give one slow breath every three seconds for about 1 minute.

8. Recheck for breathing and other signs of circulation after one minute and again every few minutes.

Signs of choking

When an infant has breathing difficulties caused by illness or an allergic reaction, get medical help urgently, or bring the infant to a hospital immediately. Do not waste time trying to clear the airway.

7

When an infant is choking, **you may see** the same signs as in an adult or child depending on the degree of obstruction.

If an infant **can breathe, cry, or cough forcefully**, the airway is clear. An infant cannot show you, as clearly as an adult, that he has trouble breathing.

Start first aid for choking immediately when you observe:

◆ the infant choking on an object
◆ weak, ineffective coughing
◆ breathing becoming faster, irregular or stopping for short periods of time
◆ high-pitched noises
◆ a bluish tinge to the skin
◆ the infant can no longer breathe, cough forcefully or cry

First aid for choking

8

When you give **first aid** for a choking infant, you should use the following **differences in procedures**:

◆ always **support** the delicate **head and neck** when holding and turning an infant
◆ **never use abdominal thrusts**
◆ give a combination of **5 back blows and 5 chest thrusts** instead
◆ use slow breaths with just enough air to make the chest rise when you try to ventilate

Remember, a baby should always receive medical care following chest thrusts and back blows to make sure there are no complications

First aid for choking

. . . .

9

Your choking infant becomes unconscious. The first aid procedures in the **correct order** are:

1. Send for medical help.

2. Look for the object.

3. Open the airway and check for breathing.

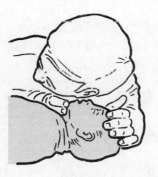

4. Attempt to ventilate (chest does not rise) reposition and try again (chest still does not rise).

5. Begin compressions - landmark and give 5 chest compressions.

6. Repeat looking for the object, attempting to ventilate and chest compressions.

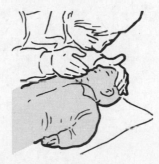

Cardiopulmonary resuscitation (CPR)

Check breathing

Check pulse

10

CPR combines two life-support skills—artificial respiration and artificial circulation.

CPR is used to circulate oxygenated blood to the tissues of an infant when –

- ◆ breathing has stopped
- ◆ the heart has stopped beating

Differences between adult and infant CPR:

- ◆ do not over extend the neck when opening the airway
- ◆ if the infant has no signs of circulation go for medical help, carry the infant with you
- ◆ use the brachial pulse
- ◆ use only two fingers for chest compressions
- ◆ compress the chest only to 1.3 to 2.5 cm (0.5 to 1 inch)
- ◆ give compressions at a rate of at least 100 per minute
- ◆ use a ratio of 5 compressions to 1 ventilation (5:1)

Chest compressions

Ventilations

11

Mark each of the following statements as either true **(T)** or false **(F)**.

- ☐ A. The first step to restore breathing is to blow in the nose and mouth.
- ☐ B. AR is an essential part of CPR.
- ☐ C. If you are alone with an unresponsive baby, your first step is to call for medical help.
- ☐ D. If breathing has stopped and there are no signs of circulation, you should start CPR immediately.
- ☐ E. You should use only one hand to give chest compressions to a baby.

Infant CPR—review

. . . .

12

You find your baby unresponsive. You have sent for medical help. The first aid procedures in the order you should do them are:

1. Open the airway and check for breathing (not breathing).

2. Try to give two slow breaths.

3. Check for signs of circulation (no signs of circulation).

4. Landmark and give compressions and ventilations for one minute.

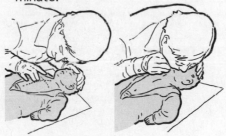

5. Recheck for signs of circulation after one minute (no signs of circulation).

6. Continue CPR.

Objectives

. . . .

CARDIOVASCULAR EMERGENCIES

AND ONE RESCUER CPR—ADULT

The heart

1

The **heart** acts as a pump. It continuously circulates blood to the lungs and all parts of the body. To do this work, it needs a steady supply of blood rich in oxygen and nutrients.

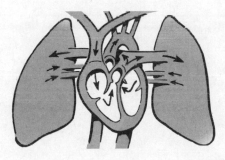

Two **coronary arteries** supply this blood to the heart muscle. If the coronary arteries or their branches become narrowed or blocked, a part of the heart will not receive the oxygen it needs. This will cause a cardiovascular emergency.

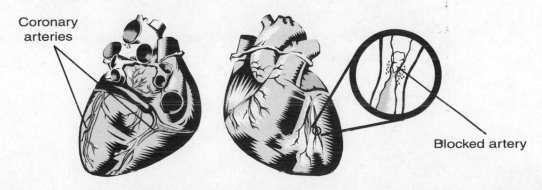

Coronary arteries

Blocked artery

Risk factors

2

A **risk factor** is a behaviour or trait that increases the chance of someone developing cardiovascular disease. Some risk factors can be controlled, while others cannot.

Cardiovascular risk factors	
Can be controlled	**Cannot be controlled**
Cigarette smoking	A person's
Elevated blood cholesterol	– Age
Elevated blood pressure	– Gender
Diabetes	– Family history
Obesity	
Lack of exercise	
Excessive stress	

The risk of developing a cardiovascular disease can be reduced considerably by adopting a healthy lifestyle.

3

Check the healthy lifestyle habits that can help control the risk of cardiovascular disease.

- ☐ A. Ensure a non-smoking environment for yourself and your family.
- ☐ B. Start an exercise program after consultation with your doctor.
- ☐ C. Eat food high in fat and calories.
- ☐ D. Have blood pressure checks by a health professional on a regular basis.
- ☐ E. Maintain a recommended body weight.
- ☐ F. Take time to relax and rest.
- ☐ G. Smoke a pipe instead of cigarettes.

Instructor-led exercise 8

· ·

4

CARDIOVASCULAR DISEASE

· · · · · · · · · · · · **High blood pressure (Hypertension)** · · · · · · · · · · · ·

1. _____ is the pressure of blood pushing against the inside walls of the blood vessels.

2. A person is said to have high blood pressure when his blood pressure is _____ above normal.

3. Two effects of high blood pressure are:

   a) The walls of the blood vessels become _____ .

   b) The heart becomes _____ .

4. The casualty with high blood pressure **always / almost never** shows signs and symptoms. *(Circle your choice.)*

· · · · · · · · · · **Narrowing of Arteries (Atherosclerosis)** · · · · · · · · · ·

5. Narrowing of arteries is caused by a build up of _____ on the inside lining.

6. The process of fat being deposited in the arteries begins: *(Circle your choice.)*

   a) when angina begins   b) in childhood   c) in middle age.

7. In the coronary arteries the build up of fatty deposits results in

   _____ .

Narrowed artery

· · · · · · · · · · · · · · · · · · **Angina** · · · · · · · · · · · · · · ·

8. Angina is a short-lived pain usually felt in the: *(Circle the correct answers.)*

   a) chest   b) neck   c) shoulders   d) jaw   e) hips   f) arms

9. Angina occurs when the heart does not get enough

   _____ to meet its needs.

10. The most common reason the heart does not get enough oxygen is that the

    arteries have become _____ .

Instructor-led exercise 8 (cont'd)

4

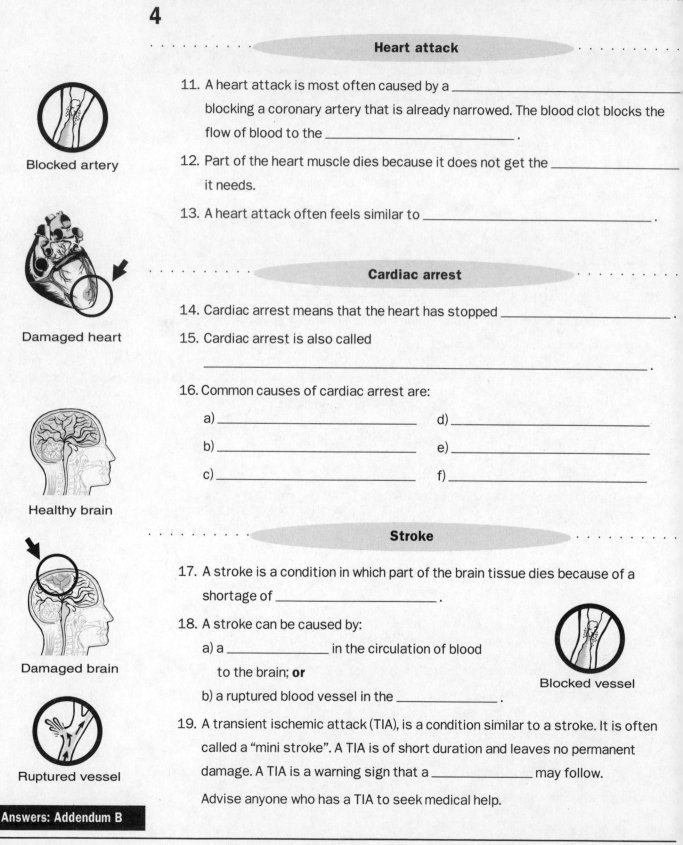

Heart attack

11. A heart attack is most often caused by a _____ blocking a coronary artery that is already narrowed. The blood clot blocks the flow of blood to the _____ .

12. Part of the heart muscle dies because it does not get the _____ it needs.

13. A heart attack often feels similar to _____ .

Blocked artery

Damaged heart

Cardiac arrest

14. Cardiac arrest means that the heart has stopped _____ .

15. Cardiac arrest is also called

_____ .

16. Common causes of cardiac arrest are:

a) _____   d) _____

b) _____   e) _____

c) _____   f) _____

Healthy brain

Stroke

17. A stroke is a condition in which part of the brain tissue dies because of a shortage of _____ .

18. A stroke can be caused by:

a) a _____ in the circulation of blood
   to the brain; **or**

b) a ruptured blood vessel in the _____ .

Blocked vessel

Damaged brain

Ruptured vessel

19. A transient ischemic attack (TIA), is a condition similar to a stroke. It is often called a "mini stroke". A TIA is of short duration and leaves no permanent damage. A TIA is a warning sign that a _____ may follow.

Advise anyone who has a TIA to seek medical help.

Angina/heart attack

5

Angina results from a temporary shortage of oxygen to the heart muscle. The signs and symptoms of angina are similar to a heart attack, except that they are often brought on by physical effort or stress and should be relieved by medication and rest. There is no heart damage in angina as there is in a heart attack.

Pain in arm

Signs and symptoms of a heart attack

The casualty may **deny** that he is having a heart attack but you may recognize some or all of the following:

You may see:

◆ shortness of breath
◆ paleness, sweating, and other signs of shock
◆ vomiting
◆ unconsciousness

Shortness of breath

The casualty may complain of:

◆ crushing chest pain which may or may not be severe
◆ pain spreading to neck, jaw, shoulders and/or arms
◆ shortness of breath
◆ fear, feeling of doom
◆ feeling of indigestion
◆ nausea

Nausea

If some or all of these signs and symptoms are present, a cardiac arrest may follow. Most heart attack deaths occur within the **first two hours** of the onset of signs and symptoms.

6

Which of the following signs and symptoms might help you to recognize angina or a heart attack? Check ☑ your answers from the listing below.

☐ A. A tingling sensation in the hands and feet.
☐ B. Breathing difficulty.
☐ C. Discomfort in the heart region.
☐ D. The casualty's insistence that it is just a stomach upset.
☐ E. A flushed face.
☐ F. White, moist skin.
☐ G. The casualty is frightened.

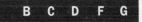

B C D F G

First aid for angina/heart attack

7

The first aid for angina and heart attack is the same.

Your aims for all cardiovascular emergencies are to:

◆ get medical help quickly

◆ reduce the workload of the heart

◆ prevent the casualty's condition from worsening

When you suspect that a person is having a heart attack or angina:

◆ get medical help **immediately**

Get medical help!

Helping the casualty to take medication

Always check the five "rights" before assisting with medications:

◆ *right medication*

◆ *right person*

◆ *right amount*

◆ *right time*

◆ *right method*

Assisting with Nitroglycerin

Only assist a casualty with medication if he is conscious and specifically asks for your help. Nitroglycerin tablets or sprays are common medications for relief of angina pain. Ask the person if he or she uses Viagra®. If the person has taken Viagra® do not assist him or her to take nitroglycerin as this may cause a significant decrease in the person's blood pressure. Ensure the medication is prescribed for this person. Spray under the tongue or place the tablets under the tongue—they aren't to be swallowed. Nitroglycerin may be repeated, if needed, every 5-10 minutes to relieve pain, or until a maximum of three doses have been taken.

◆ place the person at rest in the position of most comfort, usually **semisitting,** to ease the work of the heart and help breathing

◆ loosen tight clothing at the neck, chest and waist

◆ cover the casualty to preserve body heat

◆ reassure the casualty

◆ assist the casualty to take prescribed medication, if requested (see side bar)

◆ if the casualty's medication does not provide relief after the first dose of their medication (usually nitroglycerin), or if they have no prescribed medication, recommend the casualty chew 1 regular strength ASA tablet (325mg), or 2 childrens ASA tablets (160mg), only if they are not allergic to ASA. Research has shown that the early administration of ASA can significantly reduce the effects of a heart attack.

Assess breathing. If breathing fails, begin AR immediately.
Assess the signs of circulation. If there are no signs of circulation, begin CPR.

Cardiac arrest

8

Signs of a cardiac arrest

You will note:

◆ unresponsiveness

◆ no breathing

◆ bluish colour

◆ no signs of circulation

First aid for a suspected cardiac arrest

◆ Perform a scene survey

◆ Perform a primary survey, check ABC — airway, breathing and circulation

◆ If there are no signs of circulation, **start cardiopulmonary resuscitation (CPR) immediately**

CPR is a combination of two life-support techniques, **artificial respiration** and **artificial circulation.**

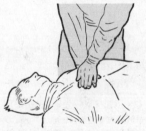

The chain of survival

CPR is important, but it is only one of the 7 steps in the **chain of survival**. Each link is as important as the others.

◆ **healthy life style choices** to prevent cardiovascular desease

◆ **early recognition** of a cardiovascular emergency

◆ **early access** to emergency medical services (EMS); this means calling for help quickly

◆ **early CPR**

◆ **early defibrillation**

◆ **early advanced care** given by medical personnel

◆ **early rehabilitation**

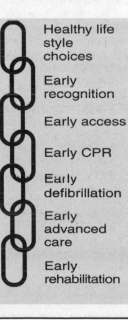

Healthy life style choices

Early recognition

Early access

Early CPR

Early defibrillation

Early advanced care

Early rehabilitation

Signs and symptoms of stroke

9

The signs and symptoms of stroke differ depending on what part of the brain was damaged. You may note some or all of the following:

You may see:

- decrease in the casualty's level of consciousness
- paralysis of facial muscles
- difficulty in speaking and swallowing, e.g. slurred speech, drooling
- unsteadiness or a sudden fall
- loss of coordination
- loss of bladder and bowel control
- unequal size of pupils

Unequal size of pupils

Paralysis of facial muscles (drooping of face)

The casualty may complain of:

- numbness or weakness of arms or legs, especially on one side
- severe headache

10

Check ☑ the signs and symptoms which could indicate that a stroke has occurred.

☐ A. The casualty wants to talk to you but cannot seem to get the words out.
☐ B. The casualty cannot move his left arm or leg.
☐ C. The casualty appears to be overactive and vomits.
☐ D. The casualty cannot control his need to urinate or move his bowels.
☐ E. When you check the pupils, they are the same size.
☐ F. You notice that the muscles on one side of the face are drooping.

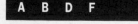

First aid for stroke

11

When you suspect that a person has had a stroke, you should **obtain medical help immediately.** Hospital treatment within one hour of the onset of symptoms will greatly increase the casualty's chances for recovery.

While waiting for medical help, you should:

◆ maintain adequate breathing and circulation

◆ protect him from injury

◆ reassure the casualty

◆ make him as comfortable as possible

◆ loosen tight clothing

If the person is **conscious:**

◆ place him at rest and support him in a **semisitting** position, unless the casualty has a weakness to one side of the body which prevents a semisitting position

◆ moisten his lips and tongue with a wet cloth, if he complains of thirst

◆ **do not offer** ASA, because of possible bleeding in the brain

If the person is **unconscious:**

◆ place him into the **recovery position** on the paralysed or weakened side to ease breathing

◆ give him nothing by mouth

If breathing stops, begin AR immediately. If circulation stops, give CPR.

Cardiovascular emergencies—review

13

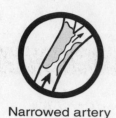

Narrowed artery

1. Depending on its location in the body, a blood vessel that is narrowed but not completely blocked, is most likely to cause which of the following cardiovascular emergencies?
Check ☑ your answers.

☐ A. TIA (transient ischemic attack—little stroke)

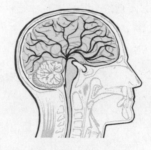

☐ B. Stroke

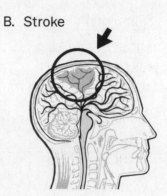

☐ C. Heart attack

☐ D. Angina

2. You have found a casualty who is not breathing and has no pulse. Which of the following illustrations shows part of the correct first aid procedures?
Check ☑ your answer.

☐ A. ☐ B. ☐ C.

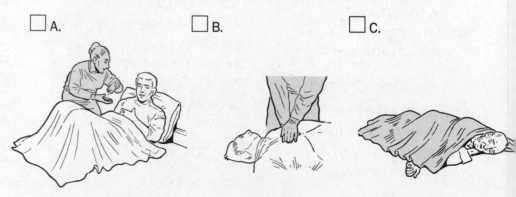

1.A 1.D 2.B

Cardiovascular emergencies—review

. . . .

14

What is happening	Signs & symptoms	First aid
Angina/Heart attack The heart muscle is not getting **enough** blood through the coronary arteries to work without pain. **Heart attack** Part of the heart muscle is not getting enough blood through the coronary arteries to keep the heart tissue alive .	Pain in the upper body. Pain may radiate. Any of the following: Denial, fear. Paleness, sweating. Nausea, indigestion, vomiting. Shortness of breath. Unconsciousness. Cardiac arrest.	Perform a scene survey. Perform a primary survey . Send or go for medical help. Place the casualty at rest in a comfortable position. Loosen tight clothing. If requested, help the casualty to take prescribed medication. Recommend the conscious casualty chew one adult ASA tablet if safe to do so. Give ongoing casualty care until medical help arrives.
Cardiac arrest The heart is not pumping any blood.	Unconsciousness. There is no breathing. There are no other signs of circulation.	Begin with a scene survey. Assess responsiveness. Send or go for medical help. Continue with a primary survey and start CPR.
Stroke A part of the brain is not getting enough blood to function properly. With a stroke, brain tissue dies . **TIA** A part of the brain is not getting enough blood to function properly. With TIA brain tissue does not die.	Changes in level of consciousness. Pupils of unequal size. Difficulty speaking and/or swallowing. Numbness or paralysis Mental confusion. Convulsions. The signs and symptoms of a TIA are not long lasting, and are not permanent.	Perform a scene survey. Perform a primary survey. Send or go for medical help. Place the casualty at rest in a comfortable position, loosen tight clothing. Give nothing by mouth. Protect the casualty during movement or convulsions. If unconscious, place in the recovery position, paralyzed side down. Give ongoing casualty care until medical help arrives .

Notes

· ·

EXERCISE 9

TWO RESCUER CPR

5 minutes

Introduction

Two people trained in two-rescuer CPR can work together as a team to give CPR. Two-rescuer CPR is not as tiring as one-rescuer CPR, and allows for continuous evaluation of the effectiveness of ventilations and compressions.

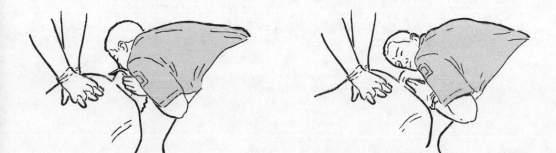

When a two-rescuer team arrives on a scene, one-rescuer CPR may, or may not, have been started. The rescue sequence for two-rescuer CPR is different in each of these scenarios. In the instructions that follow, the focus is on the different tasks of each rescuer and the communication between them.

Two-Rescuer CPR—CPR is not in Progress

2

A two-rescuer team arrives on a scene where a casualty is unconscious and CPR has not been started. Bystanders are present.

Begin ESM. Perform a scene survey

◆ As the two rescuers come on to the scene, one of the rescuers begins the scene survey taking charge, calling out for help, assessing the hazards at the scene and making the area safe. This rescuer in charge takes the role of *ventilator.*

Assess responsiveness

◆ The *ventilator* asks "Are you O.K.?" and gently taps the casualty's shoulders.
◆ The other rescuer, taking the role of the *compressor,* observes closely, ready to assist.

Send for medical help

◆ The *ventilator* sends a bystander to call for medical help.
◆ If there is no bystander, the *compressor* goes to get medical help and the *ventilator* continues with the scene survey and primary survey, giving one-rescuer CPR, if required, until the *compressor* returns.

Begin the primary survey and check for breathing

◆ The *ventilator* uses the head tilt-chin lift to open the airway and checks for breathing for up to 10 seconds.

Pinch the nose and give two slow breaths

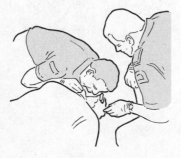

◆ The **ventilator** gives two slow breaths, remembering to:
  • keep the head tilted to maintain an open airway
  • make a good seal at the mouth and nose
  • take 2 seconds for each breath
  • watch the chest rise and fall with each breath and give time for the lungs to deflate between breaths

◆ If the chest does not rise, reposition the head and attempt to ventilate again.

2 (Continued)

Check for signs of circulation for no more than 10 seconds

◆ The *ventilator* checks for circulation, taking no more than 10 seconds.

◆ The *compressor* positions himself on the opposite side of the casualty and gets ready to give compressions. The *compressor* must:
  • landmark properly
  • put his hands in the right position on the sternum
  • be ready to give chest compressions if the **ventilator** tells him there are no signs of circulation

◆ For effective CPR, the casualty must be positioned on a firm, flat surface.

Begin compressions and give 4 cycles of 15 compressions and 2 ventilations (about one minute of CPR)

◆ If the *ventilator* finds there are no signs of circulation, he says, "Begin compressions."

◆ The *compressor* begins chest compressions, counting out loud to help maintain the rate of 100 compressions per minute. "1 and 2 and 3 and 4 and 5.....and 15"

◆ After the 15th compression, the *compressor* pauses and the *ventilator* gives 2 slow breaths. The *compressor* gives another 15 compressions, followed by 2 slow breaths from the *ventilator*. Continue CPR in cycles of 15 compressions (at a rate of 100 per minute) and 2 ventilations for one minute—about 4 cycles.

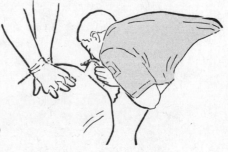

◆ While each breath is being given, the *compressor* keeps his hands in position on the casualty's chest to evaluate the effectiveness of the ventilations.

◆ While the compressions are being given, the *ventilator* monitors the carotid pulse to evaluate the effectiveness of the compressions. If no pulse is felt, the *compressor* is advised to re-landmark.

· ·

2 (Continued)

Reassess for signs of circulation

◆ After one minute of ventilations and compressions, reassess for signs of circulation

- The *ventilator* tells the compressor, "Stop compressions!"
- The *compressor* stops giving compressions, but keeps his hands in position.
- The *ventilator* checks for signs of circulation for no more than 10 seconds. If there is still no circulation, the *ventilator* says, "Resume compressions".
- The *compressor* begins giving compressions again.

◆ Continue giving CPR in cycles of 15 compressions to 2 ventilations. Reassess for signs of circulation every few minutes.

Switch Over

◆ When the *compressor* wants to change position, he gives 15 compressions and says: "Switch positions."

◆ When the *ventilator* has completed 2 breaths, the *compressor* moves to the head and takes the role of new ventilator. The *new ventilator* reassesses for signs of circulation for no more than 10 seconds and the *new compressor* landmarks for proper hand position.

◆ If there are still no signs of circulation, the *new ventilator* tells the compressor there is still no circulation. The *new compressor* gives 15 compressions.

◆ Continue CPR until the casualty's circulation returns, medical help takes over or, as a team, you are both too tired to continue.

· ·

3

Mark each of the following statements as either true **(T)** or false **(F)**.

☐ A. The compressor calls for help if no bystander is available.

☐ B. 4 cycles of 15 compressions/2 ventilations is roughly 1 minute.

☐ C. The ventilator usually calls for the switch over.

☐ D. The rate of compressions is 80 to 100 compressions per minute.

4 Two-rescuer CPR—CPR is in progress

When a two-rescuer team arrives on the scene of a cardiac arrest and one-rescuer CPR is in progress, the two-rescuer team must take over CPR in a way that ensures that the care the casualty is receiving is not interrupted. The following sequence illustrates how to do this.

Begin ESM. Perform a scene survey

◆ Once on the scene, they introduce themselves as a two-rescuer team ready to take over. They also determine if medical help has been sent for.

◆ The original rescuer moves out of the way. He goes to call for medical help if this has not been done.

Begin the primary survey

◆ The two rescuer team moves into position. The **ventilator** immediately tilts the head and checks for signs of circulation for no more than 10 seconds. At the same time, the **compressor** landmarks for proper hand position.

◆ If there are no signs of circulation the **ventilator** says, "Start compressions." The **compressor** follows with 15 compressions.

◆ Continue two-rescuer CPR.

Notes

· ·

EXERCISE 10

10 minutes

SECONDARY SURVEY

1

Once you have given first aid for life-threatening conditions, you may need to do a secondary survey.

The secondary survey is a step by step gathering of information which will help you to get a complete picture of the condition of the casualty. It also captures important information for medical help.

A secondary survey should be done when:

◆ medical help is delayed

◆ the casualty tells you about more than one area of pain

◆ you must transport the casualty to a hospital

The secondary survey consists of four steps that you should do in the following order:

1. obtain the history of the casualty
2. assess and record vital signs
3. perform a head-to-toe examination
4. give first aid for injuries and illnesses found

2

History of the casualty

By taking the history of a casualty, you are trying to find out everything that is important about the casualty's condition.

A simple way to ensure that you take a complete history of the casualty, is to remember the word **SAMPLE,** where each letter stands for a part of the history:

S = symptoms
A = allergies
M = medications
P = past and present medical history
L = last meal
E = events leading to the incident

◆ **Ask the conscious casualty** how she feels now. Be guided by the casualty's complaints

◆ If the casualty is **unconscious**, **ask relatives or bystanders** about the casualty and the situation, **check** the neck, wrist or ankles for a **medical alert device** (*see next page*)

Record the casualty's responses or any medical alert information found.

> Where do you hurt?

Medical alert information

3

A **medical alert** device, e.g. a **bracelet, necklace, anklet or pocket card** contains valuable information about the medical history of a casualty. Sometimes this information is kept in a specially marked container on the top shelf of the **person's refrigerator**. Look on the refrigerator, or front door for directions.

When examining an **unconscious** casualty **look for medical alert information.** It may help you in your assessment and in giving appropriate first aid. Some medical alert devices give a phone number where more information about the casualty can be obtained.

A medical alert device may **warn you** that the person wearing it –

◆ has a **medical condition** needing special treatment

or

◆ is **allergic** to certain substances, e.g. medications, foods, insect bites, plants

Medical alert necklace

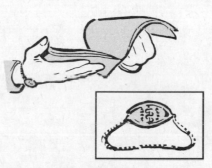

Medical alert bracelet

4

Mark each of the following statements as either true **(T)** or false **(F)**:

☐ A. Important facts that may affect the condition of a casualty may be revealed on a medical alert device.

☐ B. Medical-alert jewellery may be worn by a person who has difficulty breathing after a bee sting.

☐ C. Medical alert information will tell you the age of the casualty.

☐ D. You should also search for medical alert information on every conscious casualty.

5

Vital signs

The **vital signs** are important indicators of a casualty's condition. The four vital signs you will learn about are:

1. level of consciousness
2. breathing
3. pulse
4. skin condition

You should note and record the vital signs as a basis for further assessments.

Levels of consciousness (LOC)		

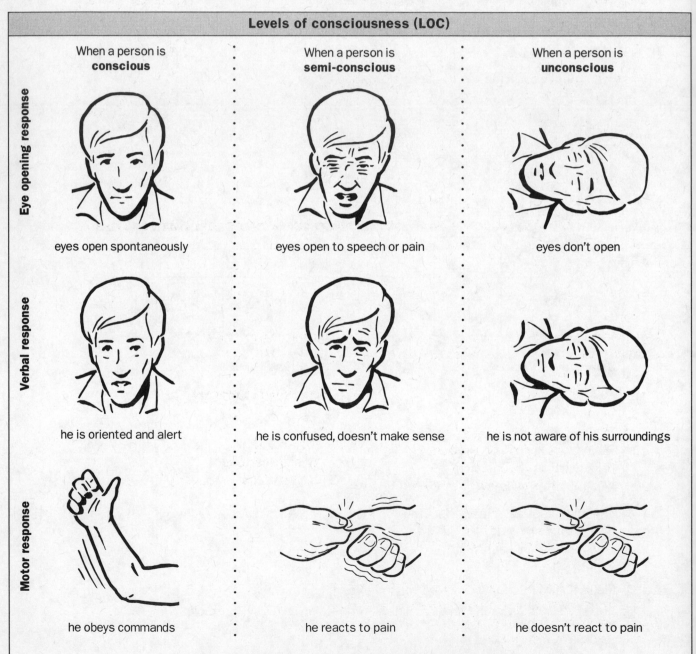

Any serious injury or illness can affect consciousness.

Levels of consciousness (cont'd)

Refer to chart with LOC on page 10 – 4

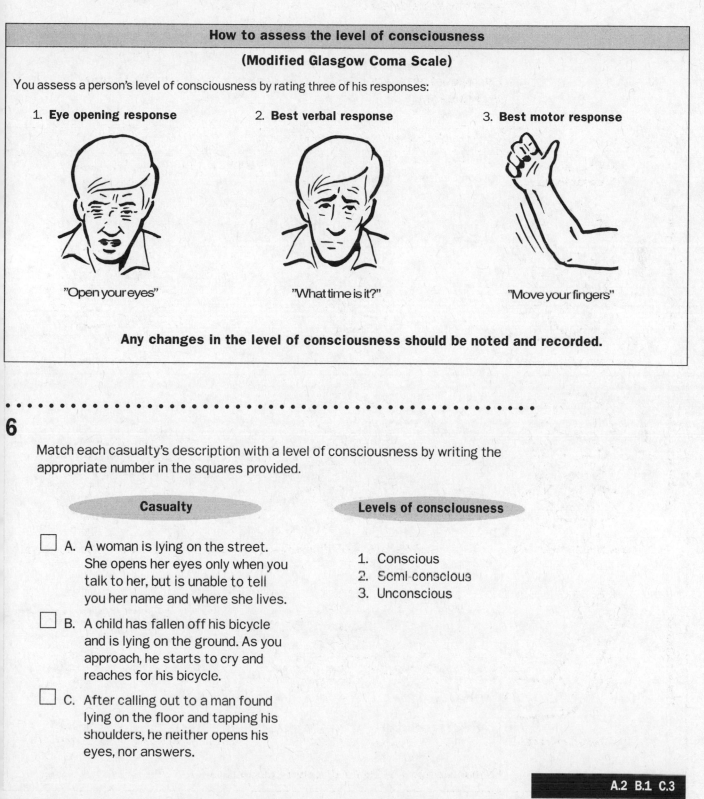

How to assess the level of consciousness

(Modified Glasgow Coma Scale)

You assess a person's level of consciousness by rating three of his responses:

1. **Eye opening response**
2. **Best verbal response**
3. **Best motor response**

"Open your eyes"
"What time is it?"
"Move your fingers"

Any changes in the level of consciousness should be noted and recorded.

6

Match each casualty's description with a level of consciousness by writing the appropriate number in the squares provided.

Casualty

☐ A. A woman is lying on the street. She opens her eyes only when you talk to her, but is unable to tell you her name and where she lives.

☐ B. A child has fallen off his bicycle and is lying on the ground. As you approach, he starts to cry and reaches for his bicycle.

☐ C. After calling out to a man found lying on the floor and tapping his shoulders, he neither opens his eyes, nor answers.

Levels of consciousness

1. Conscious
2. Semi-conscious
3. Unconscious

A.2 B.1 C.3

7

How to assess breathing

If the casualty **is conscious:**

◆ **look** at the casualty's chest/abdomen and **ask**: "Is your breathing O.K.?"

◆ **listen** to how well the casualty answers and **record** the quality (rate, rhythm and depth) of breathing

If the casualty has difficulty responding, cannot respond, or **is unconscious:**

◆ **place** a hand on the chest of the casualty and

◆ **check the rate, rhythm and depth of breathing, and record your findings**

Normal, effective breathing is quiet and effortless with an even steady rhythm. Check for:

◆ **rate** – is the number of breaths per minute within the normal range?

◆ **rhythm** – are the pauses between breaths of even length?

◆ **depth** – is the breathing shallow, too deep or gasping and noisy?

The following table gives breathing rates for all ages. If a casualty's breathing is too slow or too fast, assist breathing with artificial respiration; see page 3 – 7 in this activity book.

Breathing rate — breaths per minute			
age group	range of normal rates	too slow	too fast
adult (over 8 yrs.)	10 to 20	below 10	above 30
child (1 to 8 yrs.)	20 to 30	below 15	above 40
infant (under 1 yr.)	30 to 50	below 25	above 60

8

How to assess the pulse

The pulse is the pressure wave with each beat of the heart that is felt at different parts of the body. By taking the pulse you check that the heart is beating and blood is circulating throughout the body.

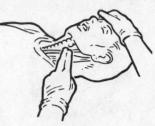

The carotid pulse

Normal pulse rates, by age	
age	rates (heartbeats per min.)
adult (8 and over)	50 to 100
child (1 to 8)	80 to 100
infant (under 1 yr.)	100 to 140

When assessing the pulse, note the:

◆ **rate** – how many times does the heart beat in a minute?

◆ **rhythm** – are the pauses regular between the pulse beats?

◆ **strength** – are the pulse beats strong or weak?

Record your findings.

The pulse of a healthy adult at rest varies from 50 to 100 beats , **averaging about 72 beats per** minute, is strong, and has a regular rhythm.

Never use your thumb

to take a pulse—it has

a pulse of its own and

you may feel it instead

of the casualty's pulse.

How to determine your own pulse rate carotid/radial:	
1. Feel your pulse	
2. Count the number of beats for 30 seconds	
3. Multiply by 2	x 2
4. The result is **your pulse rate**	

Pulse rates for an adult at rest (beats per minute)

slow	normal range		fast
40 50	60 70 72 80	90 100	110 120

↑
average

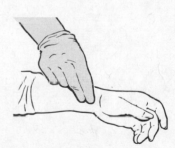

The radial pulse

Does your pulse rate fall within the **normal** range for an adult?

9

Skin condition and temperature

The condition and temperature of the skin change when there is shock. Checking skin condition and temperature will help you to find out if the casualty is in shock.

How to assess skin condition

◆ check the skin for colour –
  ❖ is it pale, reddish or bluish?
◆ check for presence of sweat –
  ❖ is the skin clammy or dry?

place the back of your hand on the forehead, neck or cheek

pull back your glove if necessary to feel change of temperature

How to assess skin temperature

◆ use the back of your hand which is more sensitive to feel –
  ❖ is the skin warm, hot or cool?
  ❖ is the skin dry or wet?

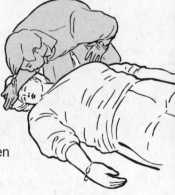

Reassess the vital signs every few minutes or when you think the casualty's condition has changed.

Write down your findings and the time of each observation.

10

To finish the secondary survey do a head to toe examination, and give first aid for any secondary injuries found.

Sample first aid report form

First Aid Report

Date _____

Location _____

First aider

Name _____

Address _____

City _____

Province _____ Postal code _____

Telephone number _____

Casualty

Name _____

Address _____

City _____

Province _____ Postal code _____

Telephone number _____

☐ Male ☐ Female Age (approx.) _____

Scene survey

Type of incident _____

Number of casualties _____
(use a separate form for each casualty)

Casualty responsiveness
☐ responsive ☐ unresponsive

Primary survey

Airway
☐ clear
☐ partly blocked
☐ completely blocked

Breathing
☐ yes.... ☐ effective ☐ ineffective
☐ no

Circulation

Pulse	☐ yes	☐ no
Severe bleeding	☐ yes	☐ no
Shock	☐ yes	☐ no

Secondary survey

History
Symptoms _____
_____
Allergies _____
Medications _____
Past medical history _____
Last meal _____
Events leading to incident _____
_____

Vital signs

Time taken	___	___	___
Level of consc.	___	___	___
Breathing rate	___	___	___
Breathing rhythm	___	___	___
Breathing depth	___	___	___
Pulse rate	___	___	___
Pulse rhythm	___	___	___
Pulse strength	___	___	___
Skin cond./temp.	___	___	___

Head-to-toe examination
Head _____
Neck _____
Collarbones _____
Shoulders arms/hands _____
Chest and under _____
Abdomen and under _____
Pelvis and buttocks _____
Legs/feet _____

First aid given

_____
_____
_____
_____

Hand over to medical help

_____
_____
_____

Notes

· ·

BONE & JOINT INJURIES
—UPPER LIMBS; MUSCLE STRAINS

Fractures

1

A basic knowledge of the structure of the upper limbs will help you to give first aid for injuries to these parts of the body.

A **fracture** is any break or crack in a bone.

A fracture may be **closed** or **open**

- **Closed fracture** – a fracture where **the skin is not broken**
- **Open fracture** – a fracture where **the skin is broken** and **bone ends may protrude**

The cause/mechanism of injury for upper limb fractures may be:

- **direct force**, e.g. a hard blow or kick
- **indirect force**, e.g. the bone breaks at some distance from the point of impact
- **twisting,** e.g. abnormal turning (rotation) of shoulder or wrist joint

Upper arm (humerus)

Forearm (radius and ulna)

Upper limb

Closed fracture

2

Mark each of the following statements as either true **(T)** or false **(F)**.

- ☐ A. There is one long bone between the shoulder and the elbow.
- ☐ B. There are two separate, long bones between the elbow and the wrist.
- ☐ C. A cracked bone over which the skin is swollen is considered an open fracture.
- ☐ D. A fracture over which a bleeding wound is seen is a closed fracture.
- ☐ E. A broken collarbone that results from a fall on the outstretched arm is caused by indirect force.

Open fracture

A.T B.T C.F D.F E.T

Joint injuries

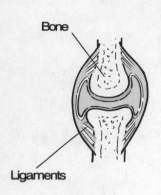

Bone

Ligaments

Joint with supporting tissue (ligaments)

3

A **joint** is formed where two or more bones come together. Joints allow for body movement. The bones of a joint are held in place by supporting tissue called **ligaments**.

The major joints of the upper limb are at the:

◆ shoulder

◆ elbow

◆ wrist

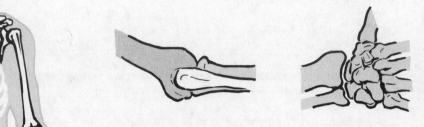

Shoulder joint   Elbow joint   Wrist joint

Joint injuries happen when the bones and surrounding tissues are forced to move beyond their normal range.

Two common joint injuries are **sprains** and **dislocations**:

◆ **sprain** – a complete or partial tearing or stretching of the ligaments around a joint

◆ **dislocation** – a displacement of one or more bone ends at a joint so that their surfaces are no longer in proper contact

4

Mark each of the following statements as either true **(T)** or false **(F)**.

☐ A. A joint is where two or more bones meet.

☐ B. Tissues surrounding the bones of a joint prevent its movement.

☐ C. A sprain occurs when the supporting tissues around a joint are over-stretched or damaged.

☐ D. A dislocation occurs when the bones at a joint are pushed out of their position.

A.T B.F C.T D.T

General signs and symptoms

5

Some or all of the following signs and symptoms occur in most bone and joint injuries –

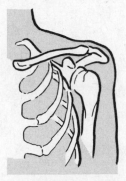
Dislocated shoulder

You may see:

◆ swelling and discolouration

◆ deformity and irregularity

◆ protruding bone ends

◆ inability to use the limb

◆ guarding and tensing of muscles around the injured area

◆ grating noise that can be heard as the bone ends rub together

◆ signs of shock, increasing with the severity of the injury

Deformity and swelling of the shoulder

The casualty may complain of:

◆ pain made worse by movement

◆ tenderness on touching

Shoulder dislocation

Open fracture of the humerus

Principles of first aid

6

The **aims of first aid** for bone and joint injuries are:

◆ to prevent further damage and reduce pain

The first aid principles to be followed are:

◆ perform a scene survey, note the mechanism of injury
◆ do a primary survey and give first aid for life-threatening injuries
◆ treat the injury at the incident site, if possible
◆ control bleeding from open wounds, if present
◆ if medical help is close by, **steady and support the injured part** in the position of greatest comfort
◆ if you are moving the casualty **immobilize** the fracture
◆ apply a cold compress, a wrapped, cold pack or ice bag on any closed fracture or injury to reduce pain and control swelling (15 minutes on – 15 minutes off)
◆ apply gentle pressure/compression with a bandage to reduce swelling of a sprain
◆ elevate the injured part, if possible
◆ monitor the casualty closely for any change in his condition
◆ reassure the casualty
◆ do not give anything by mouth
◆ give ongoing casualty care until hand over

Note: ◆ All fractures, dislocations and sprains should be immobilized before the casualty is moved, unless the casualty is in immediate danger

◆ Always immobilize in the position found.

For any closed fracture, sprain or dislocation, keep the casualty as comfortable as possible with:
◆ *R - Rest*
◆ *I - Ice*
◆ *C - Compression/ bandaging*
◆ *E - Elevation*

Position of comfort

Expose and bandage

Splinting

Muscle strains

7

A **strain** is an injury that occurs when a muscle is stretched beyond its normal limits.

The cause/mechanism of injury for a strain may be:

- sudden pulling or twisting of a muscle
- poor body mechanics during lifting
- failure to condition muscles before physical activity
- repetitive, long-term overuse

Back strain

A strain can be recognized by some or all of the following –

You may see:

- swelling of muscle
- discolouration

The casualty may complain of:

- sudden sharp pain
- severe cramps
- stiffness

Signs and symptoms may not appear until later.

Position of comfort
and cold application
for back strain

To give first aid, you should:

- place the casualty in the position of greatest comfort
- apply cold (15 minutes on – 15 minutes off) to help relax muscle spasm, reduce pain and prevent further tissue swelling
- refer to medical help

Repetitive strain injury (RSI) is a term that refers to a number of injuries, including back injuries, joint injuries, tennis elbow and bursitis. It is caused by long-term overuse of some joints, muscles and support tissue.

To give first aid:

- keep the casualty as comfortable as possible with
- rest, ice, compression and elevation—think RICE
- refer to medical help

RICE

R – rest
I – ice
C – compression/
      bandaging
E– elevation

Prevention: Work breaks, exercises, relaxation techniques, observing proper posture and use of personal protective equipment (wrist/back supports) are the keys to preventing repetitive strain injury.

Notes

· ·

BONE & JOINT INJURIES
—LOWER LIMBS

Fractures

1

A basic knowledge of the structure of the lower limbs will help you to give first aid for injuries to these parts of the body.

A **fracture** is any break or crack in a bone.

A fracture may be **closed** or **open**:

◆ **Closed fracture** – a fracture where **the skin is not broken**

◆ **Open fracture** – a fracture where **the skin is broken** and **bone ends may protrude**

The cause/mechanism of injury for lower limb fractures may be:

◆ **direct force**, e.g. a powerful force, a hard blow, a kick or a fall, especially in the elderly

◆ **indirect force**, e.g. hip fracture caused by knees forcefully striking the dashboard of a car; fracture to the kneecap caused by powerful muscle contraction

◆ **twisting,** e.g. abnormal turning (rotation) of knee or ankle—occurs in skiing or football incidents

Hip joint

Upper leg (femur)

Knee joint

Lower leg

Ankle joint

Lower limb

Closed fracture of the upper leg (femur)

Open fracture of the lower leg (tibia)

2

Mark each of the following statements as either true **(T)** or false **(F)**:

☐ A. There is one long bone between the hip and the knee.

☐ B. There are two separate, long bones between the knee and the ankle.

☐ C. A cracked bone over which the skin is swollen is considered an open fracture.

☐ D. A fracture from which a bone end is sticking out is a closed fracture.

☐ E. The thigh bone may be broken anywhere along its length.

A.T B.T C.F D.F E.T

Joint injuries

3

A **joint** is formed where two or more bones come together. Joints allow for body movement. The bones of a joint are held in place by supporting tissue called **ligaments.**

The major joints of the lower limb are at the:

◆ hip

◆ knee

◆ ankle

Bone

Ligaments

Joint with
supporting tissue
(ligaments)

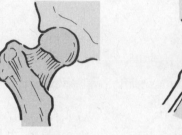

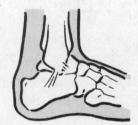

Hip joint   Knee joint   Ankle joint

Joint injuries happen when the bones and surrounding tissues are forced to move beyond their normal range.

Two common joint injuries are **sprains** and **dislocations**:

◆ **sprain** – a complete or partial tearing or stretching of the ligaments around a joint

◆ **dislocation** – a displacement of one or more bone ends at a joint so that their surfaces are no longer in proper contact

4

Mark each of the following statements as either true **(T)** or false **(F)**:

☐ A. A joint is where two or more bones meet.

☐ B. Tissues surrounding the bones of a joint prevent its movement.

☐ C. A sprain occurs when the supporting tissues around a joint are over-stretched or damaged.

☐ D. A dislocation occurs when the bones at a joint are pushed out of their position.

A.T B.F C.T D.T

General signs and symptoms

5

Some or all of the following signs and symptoms occur in most bone and joint injuries –

You may see:

◆ swelling and discolouration
◆ deformity and irregularity
◆ protruding bone ends
◆ inability to use the limb
◆ guarding and tensing of muscles around the injured area
◆ grating noise that can be heard as the bone ends rub together
◆ signs of shock, increasing with severity of the injury

The casualty may complain of:

◆ pain made worse by movement
◆ tenderness on touching

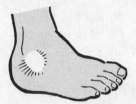

Sprained ankle deformity and swelling

Assess injury

Principles of first aid

6

The **aims of first aid** for bone and joint injuries are:

▶ to prevent further damage and reduce pain

The first aid principles to be followed are:

◆ perform a scene survey, note the mechanism of injury

◆ do a primary survey and give first aid for life-threatening injuries

◆ treat the injury at the incident site

◆ control bleeding from open wounds, if present

◆ if medical help is close by, **steady and support the injured part** in the position of greatest comfort

◆ if you must move the casualty **immobilize** the fracture

◆ apply a cold compress, a wrapped, cold pack or ice bag on any closed fracture or injury to reduce pain and control swelling (15 minutes on – 15 minutes off)

◆ apply gentle pressure/compression with a bandage for a sprain

◆ elevate the injured part, if possible

◆ monitor the casualty closely for any change in his condition

◆ reassure the casualty

◆ do not give anything by mouth

◆ give ongoing casualty care until hand over

Note: ◆ All fractures, dislocations and sprains should be immobilized before the casualty is moved, unless the casualty is in immediate danger

◆ Always immobilize in position found

For any closed fracture, sprain or dislocation, keep the casualty as comfortable as possible with:

◆ *R – Rest*
◆ *I – Ice*
◆ *C – Compression/ bandaging*
◆ *E – Elevation*

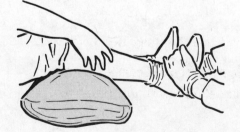

Manual support

Immobilized with a splint

Principles of Immobilization

7

Fractured bones and injured joints should be immobilized to prevent further injury and minimize pain.

If medical help is close by, you should:

◆   provide manual support to steady the injured limb until medical help arrives

Maintain support

If medical help is delayed or transport is required:

◆   immobilize an injured part to keep it from moving by using:
    ❖   splints
    ❖   slings (for upper limbs)
    ❖   bandages

Splints may be **commercially prepared** or **improvised**. An uninjured body part can also be used as a splint, e.g. a leg, the side of the body (Anatomic splint)..

A good splint should be:

◆   rigid enough to support the injured limb
◆   long enough:
    ❖   for a fracture between two joints—to extend beyond the joint above and the joint below the fracture site
    ❖   for an injured joint—for the limb to be secured so the joint can't move
◆   wide enough and padded to be comfortable

Improvised splints

When immobilization is required, follow these basic guidelines:

◆   don't do anything that causes more pain to the casualty
◆   immobilize the injured area in the position of greatest comfort
◆   check distal circulation before and after immobilization

Anatomic splint

8

Mark each of the following statements as either true **(T)** or false **(F)**:

☐   A.   Healthy body parts are unsuitable as support for broken bones.
☐   B.   A splint for a broken lower leg should extend from beyond the heel to above the knee.
☐   C.   A hockey stick could be used as a splint.
☐   D.   If the ambulance is coming shortly, help the casualty to keep her broken leg still.
☐   E.   A broken thigh should be kept aligned and still until the injury has been splinted.

A.F B.T C.T D.T E.T

Notes

· ·

HEAD/SPINAL AND PELVIC INJURIES

Introduction to head/spinal and pelvic injuries

1

A basic knowledge of the structure of **the head, spine** and **pelvis** and **how they relate to each other**, will help you to understand how injury to one part may affect the other part. It will help you to give the appropriate first aid.

Injuries to the head, spine and pelvis are always serious because of the **danger of injury to the nervous system.**

The nervous system is made up of the:

◆ brain

◆ spinal cord

◆ nerves

These delicate tissues are protected by the:

◆ skull

◆ spine

All body functions are controlled by the nervous system.

The pelvis is a basin-shaped bony structure connected to the base of the spine.

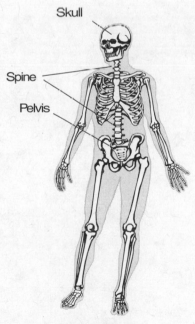

Skull

Spine

Pelvis

Full skeleton

When to suspect head/spinal injuries

∙∙

2

The **history/mechanism of injury** is the **first indication** that can lead you to suspect head/spinal injuries.

Head/spinal injuries should be suspected when a casualty:

◆ has fallen from a height or down the stairs

◆ has been in a car collision

◆ has received a blow to the head, spine or pelvis

◆ has blood or straw-coloured fluid coming from the nose or ears

◆ is found unconscious and the history is not known

The **injuries** that are commonly **associated** with a **head injury** are **neck and spinal injuries.**

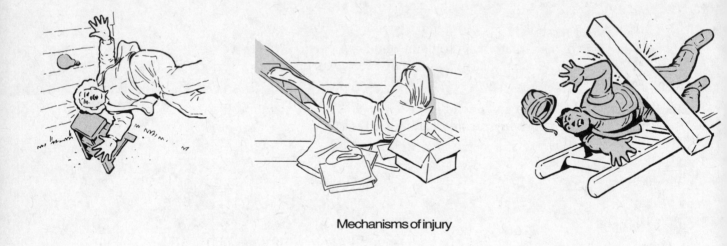

Mechanisms of injury

∙∙

3

In which of the following circumstances should you suspect that the casualty has suffered head/spinal injuries?

Check ☑ the correct answers.

☐ A. A boy hits his head when he dives into a shallow pool.

☐ B. A young person is found unconscious in bed with an empty bottle of sleeping pills on the floor.

☐ C. A heavy wooden crate falls from a hoist and hits a worker on the foot.

☐ D. During a collision, the knees of a person strike the dashboard with great force.

How to recognize head/spinal injuries

4

You can recognize head/spinal injuries by **signs and symptoms.**

You may see:

- changes in level of consciousness
- unequal size of pupils
- loss of movement of any part
- unusual lumps on the head or spine
- bruising of the head, especially around the eyes and behind the ears
- blood or straw-coloured liquid coming from the ears or nose
- vomiting

Unequal size of pupils

The casualty may complain of:

- severe pain or pressure in the head, neck or back
- tingling or loss of feeling or movement in the fingers or toes
- nausea
- headache

Checking for signs of spinal injuries

5

When you are examining a casualty, which of the following signs and symptoms may indicate head/spinal injuries? Check ☑ the correct answers.

The casualty:

- ☐ A. Has a big bump on the bony area at the back of the head.
- ☐ B. Can feel when you squeeze his hand.
- ☐ C. Can make a fist and wiggle his toes when asked to do so.
- ☐ D. Tells you of prickling sensations in his hands and feet.
- ☐ E. Doesn't know what happened and wants to throw up.
- ☐ F. Has a yellowish fluid dripping from his nose and ears.

Principles of first aid for head/spinal injuries

Don't move!

6

When a casualty has head/spinal injuries, **head or neck movement may lead to life-long disability or death.**

◆ Begin scene survey

◆ When the **mechanism of injury** suggests possible head/spinal injuries, tell the casualty **NOT TO MOVE**

◆ Offer to help and obtain consent from the conscious casualty

◆ **Send** for medical help **immediately**

Are you O.K.?

Advanced medical attention within 1 hour can help avoid permanent damage following spinal injuries

◆ **Steady and support** the head and neck in the **position found**

◆ Assess responsiveness

◆ Check the airway and for breathing

◆ If you have a bystander, show him how to steady and support the casualty's head and neck

◆ If alone, **remind the casualty not to move**

◆ Continue to perform primary survey

◆ Give first aid for life-threatening conditions

◆ Give ongoing casualty care

Firmly support the head and neck in the position found

Don't let her head move at all, and if your arms get tired, tell me.

Continue manual support of the casualty's head and neck in the position found until medical help takes over.

Keep elbows firmly supported on thighs or ground

7

Maintain an open airway

Your **first aid priority** is maintaining an open airway and adequate breathing.

If the casualty is not breathing:

◆ **open** the airway, using the **jaw-thrust without head-tilt,**
    this opens the airway without tilting the head and/or moving the neck

◆ give artificial respiration

◆ use your cheek to seal the casualty's nose if you do not have a mask to ventilate

◆ monitor breathing closely

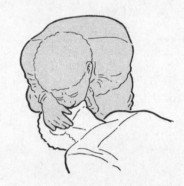

If the casualty begins to **vomit:**

◆ **steady and support the head and neck**

◆ **turn** the casualty **as a unit** onto his side with as little movement of head and spine as possible

◆ quickly clear out the mouth

◆ reposition the casualty, **supporting the head and neck at all times**

◆ reassess breathing and pulse

◆ resume ventilations if required

◆ give ongoing casualty care

◆ **continue to support the casualty's head and neck** manually until medical help takes over

8

Check ☑ the correct completions for the following statements by writing the appropriate numbers in the squares provided.

When giving artificial respiration to a casualty with a suspected neck injury –

A. The head and neck should:

    ☐ 1. Be tilted backward.
    ☐ 2. Be tilted forward.
    ☐ 3. Not be tilted.

B. When the casualty starts vomiting:

    ☐ 1. Roll the casualty to the side keeping the head and neck in the same relative position with the body.
    ☐ 2. Turn only the head quickly to the side.
    ☐ 3. Leave the casualty on her back and try to clear the mouth.

A.3 B.1

Bleeding from a scalp wound

9

Bleeding from the scalp may be severe even if the wound is superficial. Any scalp wound, depending on the mechanism of injury, could indicate a serious head injury that may cause unconsciousness and breathing problems. If you suspect head/spinal injuries, tell the casualty not to move. If a bystander is available, ask him to steady and support the head and neck in the position found.

To control bleeding from a scalp wound (no head/spinal injury suspected):

◆ perform a scene survey

◆ determine the mechanism of injury

◆ wash your hands or put gloves on, if available

◆ perform a primary survey and give first aid for life-threatening conditions

◆ clean away loose dirt from the wound

◆ avoid direct pressure, probing or contaminating the wound

◆ apply a thick, sterile dressing large enough to extend well beyond the edges of the wound

◆ hold dressing in place with a triangular bandage

◆ get medical help promptly

◆ give ongoing casualty care until hand over

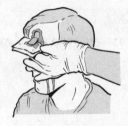

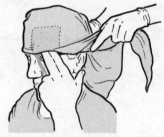

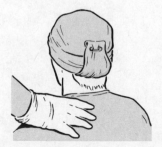

Bandaging a scalp wound

Bump on the head

10

A bump on the head is a very common injury, especially in children. It may be harmless. However, as any head injury, it should be taken seriously because of the possibility of injury to the brain.

To give first aid, for a bump on the head:

◆ be guided by the mechanism of injury

◆ if you suspect head/spinal injuries, tell the casualty not to move

◆ if you don't suspect head/spinal injuries, keep the casualty at rest

◆ put a cold compress or ice bag (15 minutes on – 15 minutes off) on the bruise to relieve pain and control swelling

◆ check the casualty often for signs of shock:

  ❖ changes in the level of consciousness (ask him questions, e.g. what his name is, where he lives)

  ❖ a change in breathing, pulse and skin temperature

  ❖ headache, nausea or vomiting

◆ check the casualty for signs of serious head injury:

  ❖ blood or straw-coloured fluid coming from the ears or nose

  ❖ seizures

  ❖ unequal pupil size

If you see any of these signs or symptoms developing, even after many days, get medical help immediately

> **⚠ Warning!**
> . . . .
> Any casualty who has lost consciousness for a few minutes should be taken to medical help. Follow medical advice on what signs and symptoms to watch for as possible indicators of a head injury.

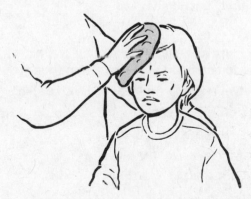

Bleeding from the ear

. . . .

11

Bleeding from the ear can have different causes. Bleeding, accompanied by a straw-coloured fluid, may indicate a fracture of the skull. To give the appropriate first aid, you have to **establish the mechanism of injury**.

If head/spinal injuries are not suspected:

- ◆ perform a scene survey
- ◆ perform a primary survey and give first aid for life-threatening conditions
- ◆ check for the cause of bleeding
- ◆ secure a dressing loosely over the ear
- ◆ place the conscious casualty semisitting, inclined toward the injured side
- ◆ place the unconscious casualty into the recovery position on the injured side
- ◆ obtain medical help
- ◆ give ongoing casualty care until hand over

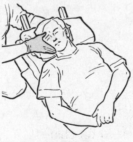

Positioning

Applying dressing

Don't move!

firmly support the head and neck in the position found and apply dressing

If head/spinal injuries are suspected:

- ◆ perform a scene survey
- ◆ tell the casualty **not to move**. If a bystander is available, ask him to **steady and support the head and neck in the position found**
- ◆ do a primary survey and give first aid for life-threatening conditions
- ◆ make no attempt to stop the flow of blood or other fluids
- ◆ do not pack the ear with gauze
- ◆ place a dressing loosely over the ear
- ◆ check breathing frequently
- ◆ obtain medical help immediately
- ◆ give ongoing casualty care until medical help takes over

Head/spinal injuries—review

12

1. Which of the following illustrations show a mechanism of injury that would indicate possible head/spinal injuries? Check ☑ your answers.

    ☐ A.

    ☐ B.

    ☐ C.

    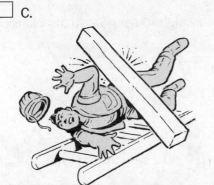

    ☐ D.

    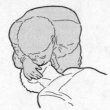

2. If you suspect head/spinal injuries, which of the following illustrations shows the right way to open the airway? Check ☑ your answer.

    ☐ A. Jaw-thrust without head-tilt

    ☐ B. Head-tilt chin-lift

3. Which of the following illustrations shows the best positioning for a conscious casualty with head/spinal injuries? Check ☑ your answer.

    ☐ A.

    ☐ B.

    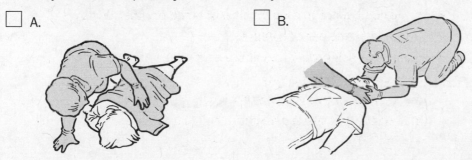

When to suspect a pelvic injury

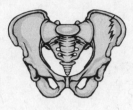

13

A **pelvic injury** is any break or crack in the bones of the pelvis.

When arriving at an emergency scene, look for the causes and the history of the incident. Try to find out what happened to the casualty and how much force was involved.

The mechanism of injury for a pelvic injury is usually:

◆ **direct force,** e.g. a direct crush or heavy impact and may involve injury to the organs in the pelvic area, especially the bladder

◆ **indirect force,** e.g. in a fall, the force is applied to the pelvis through the legs or hip joints, or by pulling or twisting

In the elderly, even a simple fall may cause a fracture in the pelvic area.

Mechanisms of injury

Signs and symptoms of a pelvic injury

14

If the pelvis has been injured –

You may see:

◆ signs of shock (internal bleeding may be present)

◆ inability of the casualty to stand or walk

◆ inability to urinate or bloody urine

The casualty may complain of:

◆ sharp pain in the hips, groin and the small of the back

◆ increased pain when moving

◆ urge to urinate

An injury of the pelvis may result in damage to the **lower spine** or to the **bladder,** leading to serious infection.

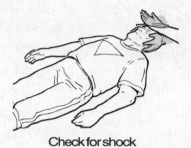

Check for shock

Check abdomen

Check lower back

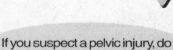

Check pelvis

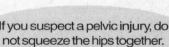

If you suspect a pelvic injury, do not squeeze the hips together.

Principles of first aid for a pelvic injury

15

A **pelvic injury** is often **associated with a spinal injury** and should be treated with the same care as a spinal injury:

◆ begin scene survey

◆ when the mechanism of injury suggests a pelvic injury, tell the casualty **NOT TO MOVE**

◆ offer to help and obtain consent from the conscious casualty

◆ send for medical help immediately

◆ steady and support the casualty in the position found

◆ assess responsiveness

◆ check the airway and for breathing

◆ if there is a bystander, show him how to steady and support the casualty

◆ if alone, remind casualty not to move

◆ continue with the primary survey, check for circulation

◆ give first aid for any life-threatening condition

◆ **support both sides of the pelvis with heavy padded objects to prevent movement**, e.g. weights rolled in blankets, if possible

◆ give ongoing casualty care

Continue to support the casualty manually until medical help takes over.

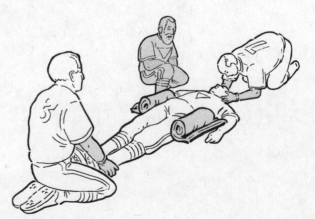

First aid for pelvic injuries—review

16

A baseball player was hit with a baseball bat in his lower back. He complains about sharp pain in the hips and in the small of the back. There are several bystanders ready to help.

Based on the history and mechanism of injury, the correct first aid procedures for this casualty, **in the order you should perform them are:**

1. Take charge.

Don't move!
Can I help?
Get medical help.

2. Steady and support head and neck.

3. Check the airway.

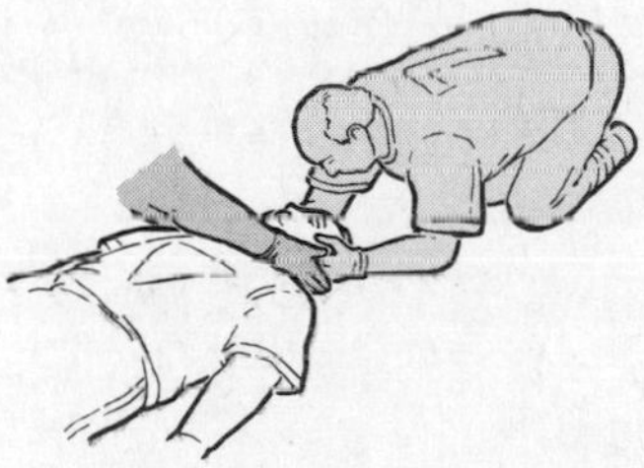

4. Check breathing.

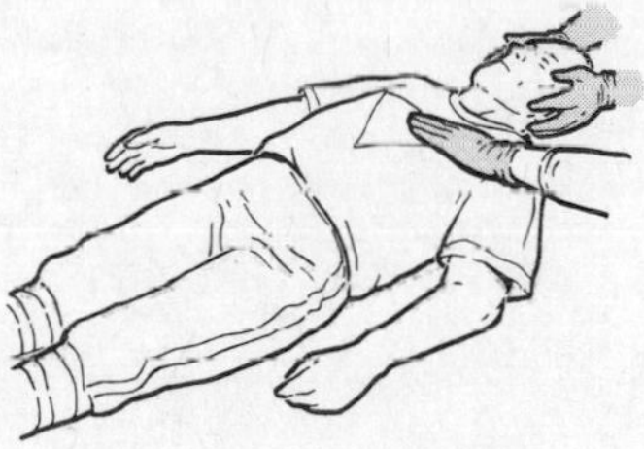

5. Check for shock.

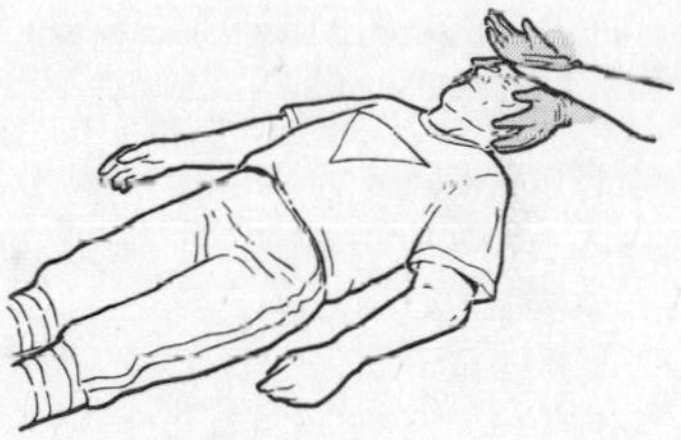

6. Do a rapid body survey.

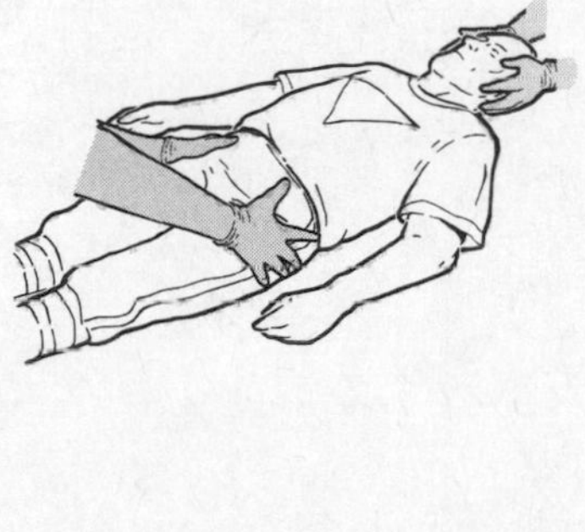

7. Support the pelvis.

8. Give ongoing casualty care.

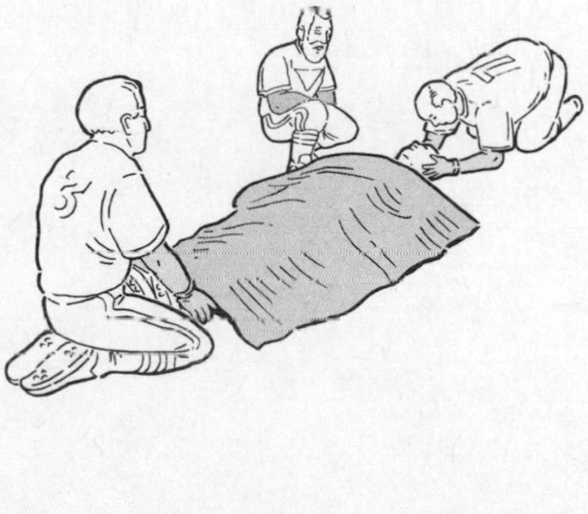

Notes

CHEST INJURIES

Introduction to chest injuries

1

A basic knowledge of the structures of the chest will help you to give first aid for injuries in this area. The **chest cavity** is formed by the:

◆ breastbone (sternum)

◆ ribs

◆ spine

These bones protect the **lungs**, **heart** and **major blood vessels.**
The chest cavity is separated from the abdominal cavity by the **diaphragm.**

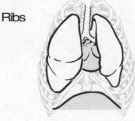

Breastbone

Ribs

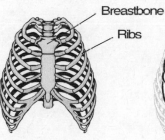

Chest cavity

Chest cavity, inside view

Blunt force

There are two general types of chest injuries:

◆ **closed** – the skin remains unbroken (usually caused by a blunt force)

◆ **open** – the skin is broken (when the chest is punctured)

Chest injuries **can be life-threatening** because of the possibility of –

◆ severe breathing problems

◆ damage to the heart and lungs

◆ internal bleeding

Knife wound

Penetrating chest wound

2

A penetrating or "sucking" chest wound occurs when an object punctures the chest. Through the open chest wound **air enters** directly into the chest cavity instead of through the airway into the lungs, causing serious breathing problems.

Some or all of the following signs and symptoms may be present –

You may observe:

◆ sounds of air being sucked into the chest when the casualty breathes in

◆ blood-stained bubbles at the wound site when the casualty breathes out

◆ coughing up of frothy blood

◆ inability to expand one or both sides of the chest

◆ laboured breathing

◆ signs of shock

The casualty may complain of:

◆ pain during breathing

A penetrating chest wound **can be life-threatening**. The aim of first aid is to restore effective breathing immediately.

Knife wound

Gunshot wound

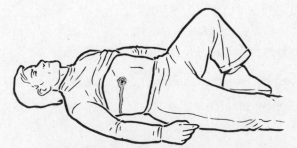

Penetrating chest wound with blood-stained bubbles

First aid for a penetrating chest wound—review

3

The steps below in **the correct order of performance** are:

1. Preform a scene survey, then check airway and breathing.

2. Expose the wound.

3. Cover the wound with the casualty's hand.

4. Check circulation (shock) and perform a rapid body survey.

5. Position the casualty. Cover the wound with an airtight dressing and tape on three sides.

6. Give ongoing casualty care. Check the dressing frequently to ensure air can escape.

Flail chest

· ·

4

A **flail chest** results when several ribs in the same area are broken in more than one place. The **mechanism of injury** may be a severe blow or a crushing force to the chest, e.g. a car crash, a fall or being struck by a large object.

Body hits steering wheel

Blunt force

A flail chest may be recognized by the following –

You may see:

◆ abnormal movement of the injured part of the chest wall during breathing

◆ laboured, ineffective breathing

◆ bruising at the injury site

The casualty may complain of:

◆ pain during breathing

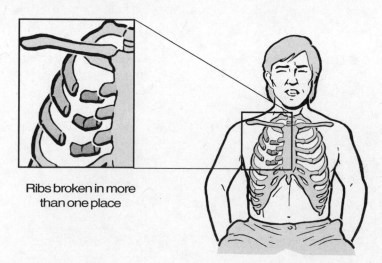

Ribs broken in more than one place

Flail chest

First aid for a flail chest

5

The force that caused a flail chest may have also caused head/spinal injuries.

As soon as you suspect major injuries, give first aid as for a casualty with suspected head/spinal injuries:

◆ tell the casualty not to move

◆ obtain medical help

◆ leave the casualty in the position found and support the head and neck

◆ perform a primary survey, check airway and breathing

◆ if the casualty complains of difficulty breathing and pain in the chest, expose and examine the injury. Hand support over the injury may make breathing easier

◆ do not apply padding over the area or wrap bandages around the chest

◆ give first aid for ineffective breathing if needed

◆ continue your primary survey, check circulation

◆ give ongoing casualty care until medical help takes over

6

A conscious casualty of a head-on collision has difficulties breathing and shows signs and symptoms of a flail chest. An ambulance has been called. What first aid should you give until medical help takes over?

Check ☑ the correct answers.

☐ A. Ensure that the casualty is not moving.

☐ B. Check breathing and help the casualty to breathe if required.

☐ C. Bandage a firm pad over the flail area.

☐ D. Place the casualty into a semisitting position.

A   B

Closed fracture of the rib cage

· ·

7

Closed fractures of one or more ribs may show no signs of external injury and are not usually life-threatening. The mechanism of injury is commonly a direct blow to the chest.

Guarding

You may observe:

◆ shallow, uncoordinated breathing
◆ bruising or deformity at the suspected fracture site
◆ guarding
◆ grating sound on movement
◆ if lungs are punctured by the broken ribs, casualty may cough up frothy blood and have increased difficulty breathing

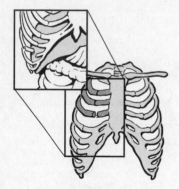

Closed fracture of the rib cage

The casualty may complain of:

◆ pain at the fracture site that increases with movement

To give first aid, you should:

◆ perform a scene survey
◆ perform a primary survey
◆ expose and examine the injury site if the casualty has difficulty breathing. Hand support over the injured area may make breathing easier
◆ place the conscious casualty in a semisitting position, inclined toward the injured side to help breathing
◆ support the arm on the injured side in a St. John tubular sling. This will transfer the weight of the arm to the uninjured side
◆ obtain medical help
◆ give ongoing casualty care until hand over to medical help

Positioning

Note: If the casualty shows severe breathing difficulties and signs of shock, give first aid as for a flail chest

Blast injury

8

The violent shock waves from an explosion can seriously damage the lungs and internal organs. Even when there is no sign of other injury, a life-threatening breathing emergency can result from a blast injury.

To assess a blast injury, consider:

◆ the mechanism of injury (type and extent of explosion, casualty's closeness to the explosion)
◆ the signs and symptoms of the casualty

You may see:

◆ frothy blood being coughed up
◆ laboured breathing
◆ signs of shock

The casualty may complain of:

◆ chest pain

To give first aid for a blast injury:

◆ perform a scene survey
◆ immobilize the casualty's head and neck, if head and spinal injury are suspected
◆ if the casualty is unconscious, get medical help immediately
◆ perform a primary survey and give first aid for life-threatening injuries
◆ give assisted breathing, if required
◆ assist the conscious casualty to a semisitting position to ease breathing
◆ place the unconscious casualty into the recovery position
◆ give ongoing casualty care until medical help takes over

Wave of explosion

Notes

· ·

WOUND CARE

Wounds

1

A **wound** is any break in the **soft tissues** of the body.

A wound can be either open or closed:

◆ **open wound** – there is a break in the outer layer of the skin. It results in bleeding and may permit the entrance of germs that cause infection

◆ **closed wound** – there is no break in the outer layer of the skin. There is no external bleeding and little risk of infection. Soft tissue damage occurs under the skin, e.g. a bruise.

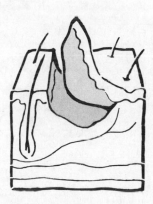
Open wound

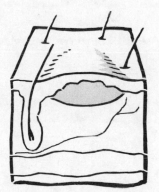
Closed wound

The aims in the care of wounds are to:

◆ stop bleeding
◆ prevent further contamination and infection

Contamination and infection

2

Contamination (germs, dirt or foreign material) in an open wound may lead to **infection**. All open wounds are contaminated to some degree.

Prevent further contamination of an open wound. Follow these steps for cleansing a minor wound:

◆ wash your hands with soap and water or use clean gloves, if possible, before giving first aid

◆ do not cough or breathe directly over the wound

◆ do not touch the wound

◆ gently wash the wound under slowly running water if there is loose material on the surface

◆ protect the wound with a temporary, preferably sterile or clean, dressing

◆ wash surrounding skin with clean swabs. Wipe away from the wound

◆ dry surrounding skin with clean swabs. Wipe away from the wound

◆ remove temporary dressing

◆ cover the wound promptly with a sterile or clean dressing and tape in place

◆ remove and dispose of gloves when wound care is completed

◆ wash your hands and any other skin area that has been in contact with the casualty's blood

Wound infection

Any wound that becomes infected should be seen by a doctor. Recognize infection in a wound when the wound:

◆ becomes more painful

◆ becomes red and perhaps swollen

◆ feels warmer than the surrounding area

◆ shows the presence of pus (whitish fluid)

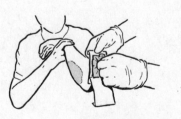

Clean a wound

Cover a wound

Remove gloves

Tetanus infection

3

Any open wound can be contaminated with a bacterial spore that causes **tetanus (lockjaw)**.

Tetanus is a serious disease that can be fatal. It is characterized by muscle spasms and stiffness of the jaw. The tetanus germ is found in soil, dust and animal feces. Particular care should be taken with wounds caused by farming or gardening tools and rusty nails. Careful washing can flush away the bacillus before it can cause infection in minor wounds. Deep wounds are at high risk for tetanus infection.

As a first aider, **it is your duty to advise any casualty with an open wound to protect himself against tetanus** by seeing a doctor as soon as possible.

A person can be protected against tetanus by immunization.

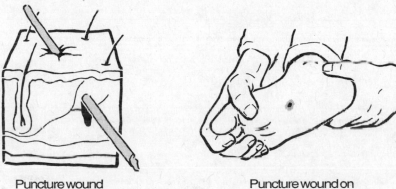

Puncture wound

Puncture wound on sole of foot

4

Mark each of the following statements as either true **(T)** or false **(F)**.

☐ A. Tetanus infection is a threat only if a wound is caused by rusty metal.
☐ B. The tetanus germ grows best in deep wounds.
☐ C. The tetanus germ can infect the body through the food we eat.
☐ D. The disease, also called lockjaw, can result in death.
☐ E. Deep wounds with dirt inside should be checked by a doctor following first aid.

Dressing, bandages and slings

5

Improvised dressings

Commercial dressings

Commercial bandages

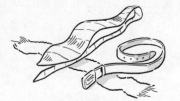

Improvised bandages

Dressings and **bandages** are basic tools of first aid.

A dressing is a protective covering placed on a wound to help control bleeding, to absorb blood from a wound and to prevent further contamination and infection.

A dressing should be:

◆ sterile or as clean as possible

◆ highly absorbent to keep the wound dry

◆ thick, soft and compressible so that pressure can be applied evenly over the affected area

◆ non-stick and lint-free to reduce the possibility of sticking to the wound

  ❖ gauze, cotton or linen make good dressings

◆ large enough to completely cover the wound

A bandage is a material used to:

◆ hold dressings in place

◆ maintain pressure over a wound

◆ support a limb or joint

◆ immobilize parts of the body

◆ secure a splint

The **triangular bandage** is the most versatile bandage and may also be used as a:

◆ ring pad

◆ arm sling

◆ St. John tubular sling

Dressings and bandages can be **commercially prepared** or **improvised**.

Triangular bandage

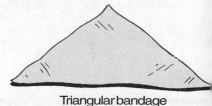

Broad bandage

6

Several choices for improvised dressings and bandages are described below.

Check ☑ the ones you could safely use.

☐ A. A piece of clean bed linen large enough to cover a wound.

☐ B. A cotton towel cut to size to extend over the edges of a wound.

☐ C. Fluffy cotton balls make a good covering for a wound.

☐ D. A belt can be used as an improvised sling.

☐ E.. A large garbage bag can be made into a sling.

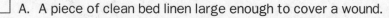

A B D E

Bleeding from the nose

. . . .

7

A nosebleed may occur spontaneously or may be caused by:

◆ blowing the nose

◆ injury to the nose or skull

To control a nosebleed, you should:

◆ do a scene survey

◆ do a primary survey

◆ place the casualty in a sitting position with the head slightly forward

◆ tell the casualty to **pinch the soft parts of the nose firmly** with the thumb and forefinger for **about 10 minutes** or until bleeding stops

◆ loosen tight clothing around the casualty's neck and chest

◆ keep the casualty quiet to avoid increased bleeding

◆ get medical help if bleeding does not stop or if bleeding recurs

◆ when bleeding stops, tell the casualty **not to blow his nose** for a few hours

Do not try to stop a nosebleed caused by a head injury!

If the mechanism of injury indicates a possible head injury, you should:

◆ steady and support the head and neck

◆ wipe away the external trickling blood do not try to stop it and do not poke the nostrils with tissues

◆ call for medical help immediately

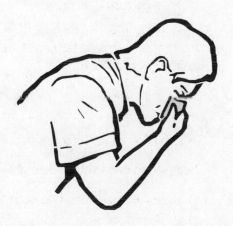

Bleeding from the gums, tongue and cheek

8

Bleeding from the gums, tongue or cheek can occur following a tooth extraction, a knocked out tooth or other injury and can be very heavy.

There is a danger of the blood entering the airway causing choking, or the stomach causing nausea:

◆ **always ensure an open airway**

Give first aid for bleeding from the gums as follows:

◆ wash hands and put gloves on

◆ place a gauze pad firmly on the tooth socket or injury site. Use a pad thick enough to keep the teeth apart when biting

◆ ask the casualty to bite on the pad until the bleeding stops and to support the chin with his hands, if possible

◆ obtain medical or dental advice if bleeding cannot be controlled

◆ do not wash out the mouth after bleeding has stopped. It may disturb clots and cause bleeding to resume

If a tooth has been knocked out, do not touch the roots. Gently place it in a cup of milk and see a dentist immediately. If milk is not available, the tooth may be preserved in a saline solution or wrapped in plastic wrap kept moist with the casualty's saliva.

Give first aid for bleeding from the tongue and cheek as follows:

◆ wash hands and put on gloves

◆ use a sterile dressing or clean cloth and compress the bleeding part between the finger and thumb until the bleeding stops

Bleeding tongue

Bleeding cheek

A bleeding gum should be treated as a sign of a boken jaw until proven otherwise

Knocked out tooth

Abdominal injuries

9

The **abdomen** is the body area below the chest.

The **abdominal cavity** is the space between the diaphragm and the lower part of the pelvis. This cavity contains the abdominal organs, e.g. stomach, liver, spleen.

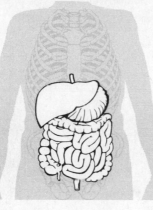

An injury to the abdomen may be a **closed wound** or an **open wound**.

Closed wounds are those in which the abdomen is injured but the skin remains unbroken. The mechanism of injury could be, e.g. a severe blow or a crush injury.

Open wounds are those in which the skin is broken. The mechanism of injury could be, e.g. a puncture wound or a cut with a knife.

Closed and open wounds of the abdomen may result in injuries to the internal organs.

First aid for abdominal wounds

10

Any abdominal wound should be treated as a serious condition because there is a danger of:

◆ **severe internal bleeding** from damaged organs
◆ **contamination** from the contents of the ruptured organs

This may lead to:

◆ **severe shock**
◆ **infection**

An open abdominal wound may allow internal organs to protrude.

To give first aid for an open abdominal wound:

◆ consider the history and mechanism of injury
◆ prevent the wound from opening wider by positioning the casualty with head and shoulders slightly raised and supported, and knees raised

Internal organs not protruding:

◆ apply a dry dressing
◆ bandage firmly over the dressing
◆ give nothing by mouth
◆ obtain medical help immediately

Semisitting

Apply dressing

Tape dressing

11

Internal organs protruding:

◆ do not replace organs

◆ apply a large, moist, sterile dressing to prevent drying of the organs

◆ secure dressings without pressure

◆ give nothing by mouth

◆ obtain medical help immediately

◆ if the casualty is coughing or vomiting, support the abdomen with two broad bandages

◆ give ongoing casualty care until medical help takes over

Expose area

Semisitting

Place moist dressings

Tape dressings in place

Apply broad bandages

12

From the choices below, check ☑ the correct first aid procedures for a conscious casualty with an abdominal wound.

☐ A. Gently push the organs back into the abdomen.

☐ B. If the casualty complains of thirst, give sips of water.

☐ C. Give nothing to eat or drink.

☐ D. If the casualty starts to vomit, apply more bandages to prevent further opening of the wound.

☐ E. Cover the wound with a dressing and secure in place.

Notes

· ·

MULTIPLE CASUALTY MANAGEMENT

Triage

. . . .

1

When the number of **casualties is greater than the number of first aiders,** you must decide in which order the injured should get **first aid**, and which casualties should be taken to **medical help** first. This process of decision making is called triage.

Triage is the process of sorting and classifying casualties by assigning **priorities** of **first aid** and **transportation** for all the injured.

Multiple casualty scene

1 (cont'd)

If you are alone, perform the scene survey and a complete primary survey, including first aid for immediate life-threatening problems, in turn on all casualties.

The mechanism of injury will help you decide to which casualty you should go first.

Ensure the following:

A – An open airway; with support of head and neck, if head/spinal injuries are suspected

B – Breathing, to allow for adequate ventilation

C – Circulation, including control of severe bleeding and first aid for shock

Remember, each casualty should be examined and given first aid for these life-threatening conditions before any other injuries are cared for.

Head injuries

Stopped breathing

Severe bleeding

Priorities

2

The **sorting and assigning of priorities** should be done as soon as you can do so safely. Casualties are usually sorted into **three levels** according to their priorities of emergency care.

Highest priority—those casualties requiring immediate first aid and transportation because of:

◆ airway and breathing difficulties

◆ no signs of circulation, if sufficient first aiders are available to give first aid for other life-threatening conditions

◆ severe bleeding

◆ shock

◆ severe head injuries

◆ severe burns

◆ severe medical problems, e.g. poisoning, diabetes and cardiovascular emergencies

◆ open chest or abdominal wounds

Second priority—those casualties who probably can wait one-hour for medical help without risk to their lives:

◆ burns

◆ major or multiple fractures

◆ back injuries (with or without spinal damage)

Lowest priority—those casualties who may receive first aid and transportation last:

◆ minor fractures

◆ minor bleeding

◆ behavioural problems

◆ no signs of circulation, if enough first aiders are not available

◆ obviously dead

3

An industrial explosion has caused serious injuries to four workers. Following the scene survey, you note that all are conscious. One worker is bleeding profusely. Another worker has painful burns on his arms. The third is pale, sweating and showing signs of shock, and the fourth seems hysterical.

If alone, in which order would you give first aid to these casualties? Place the appropriate number in the boxes provided.

☐ A. The worker who is burned.

☐ B. The worker who is bleeding profusely.

☐ C. The worker who is in shock.

☐ D. The worker who is walking around screaming.

B.1 C.2 A.3 D.4

4

Your ability to save lives depends on your knowledge and skills to evaluate which casualties need immediate first aid and which casualties can wait without being harmed further. Trust your own judgement and do what is best for most casualties.

Procedures to follow:

- ◆ if there **is more than one first aider** at the scene, the most knowledgeable first aider should take charge and do the triage
- ◆ complete a primary survey on each casualty first and give first aid for immediate life-threatening problems
- ◆ call for additional assistance if needed
- ◆ assign available first aiders and equipment to the highest priority casualties
- ◆ transport the highest priority casualties and those that are stabilized first
- ◆ reassess casualties regularly for changes in their condition

When you are caring for one or more casualties, remember that:

- ◆ **assigned priorities for giving first aid and transportation should be reviewed often. They should be changed if any of the casualties' conditions require more urgent care.**

5

You are applying direct pressure to a severely bleeding wound of the conscious casualty's leg. Suddenly another casualty starts gasping for air and stops breathing. What should you do?

From the following options, check ☑ the correct answer.

- ☐ A. Continue giving first aid to the bleeding casualty.
- ☐ B. Show the bleeding casualty how to keep pressure on his wound and immediately give first aid to the casualty who has stopped breathing.
- ☐ C. Call out for help and wait for a bystander who could assist you.
- ☐ D. Bandage the bleeding wound to maintain pressure and elevate the arm in a sling before you give first aid to the non-breathing casualty.

Lightning injuries

7

Casualties with **no signs of circulation** are normally assigned the lowest priority, unless there are enough first aiders available to give first aid to all casualties.

Lightning injuries are an exception to this rule—**reverse usual triage procedures:**

◆ if someone has been struck by lightning, give first aid for the **apparently dead first**. Casualties of a lightning strike have a greater chance of being revived than a casualty whose heart has stopped because of other causes

Follow these steps

◆ Perform a scene survey and make the area safe, e.g. broken trees, glass

Note: Persons who are struck by lightning are safe to handle. There is no danger of being electrocuted by touching them.

◆ Get a brief history and establish the mechanism of injury

◆ Steady and support the casualty's head and neck to prevent a possible spinal injury from becoming worse

◆ Perform a primary survey

◆ Begin CPR to maintain breathing and circulation

The key to survival is an early, vigorous and prolonged resuscitation effort

◆ Once circulation is restored, monitor breathing and pulse continuously. The casualties may arrest again

◆ Give ongoing casualty care until hand over to medical help

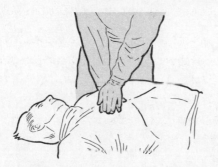

Notes

· ·

RESCUE CARRIES

Principles of safety for moving a casualty

1

In most emergency situations, **do not move a casualty**, except for reasons of safety. Moving a casualty poses dangers to the first aider as well as to the casualty. However, there are times when you have to move a casualty **for safety or essential life-saving first aid.**

Before you try to move an injured person, consider the following **principles of safety:**

◆ select the method that will pose the least risk to yourself and the casualty

◆ you can be of little help to a casualty if you injure yourself in the rescue

◆ only try to move a casualty you are sure you can safely handle

◆ **support and immobilization** of the injuries should be provided before and during the move

◆ move a casualty the shortest possible distance

◆ use as many bystanders as you need to keep risks to a minimum

Ensure safety at the scene

2

In which of the following situations should you try to move a casualty before giving first aid?

Check ☑ the correct answers.

☐ A. A mechanic is lying inside a burning car.

☐ B. An elderly man is found unconscious on the sidewalk.

☐ C. A woman is lying in a ditch of water with her face submerged.

☐ D. A teenager is lying at the foot of a long stairway.

☐ E. A child is floating on the lake under an overturned boat.

Lifting techniques

3

When lifting and transporting heavy objects, such as a casualty, protect yourself from injury. Rescuers often suffer muscle strain caused by using incorrect body mechanics when lifting and moving a casualty.

You should use proper body mechanics:

When lifting –

◆ stand close to the casualty

◆ bend your knees; do not stoop

◆ get a good grip on the casualty or equipment

◆ lift, using the thigh, leg and abdominal muscles, and keeping your back straight

◆ when turning, follow your feet, do not twist your body

Ensure that rescuers lift together on a signal.

When lowering –

◆ reverse the procedure

◆ remember that poor body mechanics can exert extreme pressure on the lower back and may cause muscle and disc injuries

If the rescuers are unskilled, practise the proper techniques before moving the casualty.

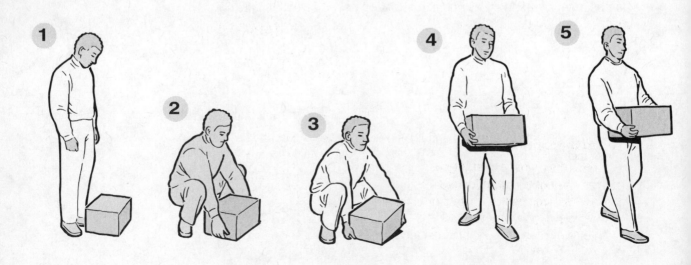

One-rescuer carries

4

When you are alone and you must move a casualty, use one of the following rescue carries:

- ◆ **pick-a-back**
  - ❖ to carry a lightweight casualty who cannot walk but who can use his upper limbs

- ◆ **cradle carry**
  - ❖ to carry a child or lightweight adult who is unable to walk

- ◆ **human crutch**
  - ❖ to support a casualty who has one injured lower limb but can walk with help or someone who feels ill

Two-rescuer carries

5

When you must move a casualty and you have a helper, use one of the following rescue carries:

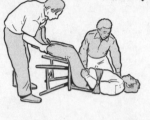

◆ **chair carry**

❖ to transport either a **conscious** casualty who cannot walk, or an **unconscious** casualty through hallways or up and down stairways (a third rescuer should assist when transporting on stairs)

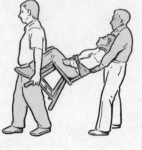

◆ **two-hand seat**

❖ to carry a conscious casualty who can neither walk nor support his upper body

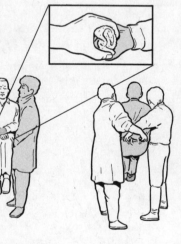

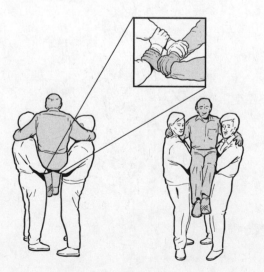

◆ **four-hand seat**

❖ to carry a conscious casualty who has the use of both arms but cannot walk

Blanket lift

. . . .

6

The **blanket lift** is used by a team of rescuers (at least four) to carry a helpless or unconscious casualty. Before attempting this lift, be sure to **test the blanket**. Ensure that it will carry the casualty's weight safely.

Do not use this lift if you suspect the casualty has head / spinal injuries.

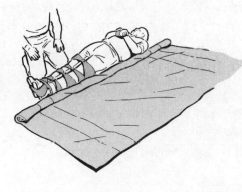

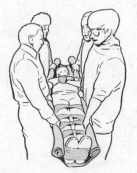

Drag carry

. . . .

7

In some situations, a casualty with suspected head/spinal injuries may be in immediate danger. If you are alone, move this casualty to safety using the **drag carry**. A drag carry involves **dragging** the casualty while **providing protection for the head and neck.**

You should do the following:

◆ stand at the casualty's head facing his feet

◆ crouch down

◆ ease your hands under the casualty's shoulders and grasp his clothing on each side

◆ steady and support the casualty's head and neck on your forearms

◆ move backward carefully and **drag** the casualty **lengthwise** only as far as necessary for safety

◆ if time permits, secure the casualty's hands together across his chest before dragging

Drag carry

Forward drag carry

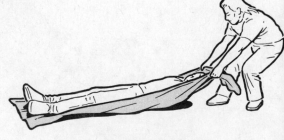

Drag carry on blanket

Drag carry from a sitting position

. . . .

8

To remove **a sitting casualty** with suspected head/spinal injuries **from a life-threatening situation**, e.g. from a car, you should proceed as follows:

◆ free the feet and legs

◆ ease your forearm under the person's armpit on the exit side . Extend your hand to support the casualty's chin

◆ ease the casualty's head gently backward to rest on your shoulder while **keeping the neck as rigid as possible**

◆ ease your other forearm under the armpit on the opposite side and grasp the wrist of the casualty's arm nearest the exit

◆ establish a firm footing and swing around with the casualty

◆ drag the casualty from the vehicle to the closest safe distance, with the least possible twisting of the casualty's spine

Drag carry from a sitting position

Notes

· ·

EYE INJURIES

Structure of the eye

1

The **eye** is the **very delicate** organ of sight. To give safe and appropriate care, you should know the **basic structure of the eye**.

Eyeball – fluid-filled globe which is the main part of the eye

Cornea – thin, transparent front of the eyeball that allows light to enter the eye

Eyelid   – movable layers of skin that provide a protective covering for the eye

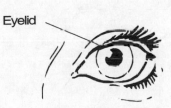
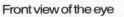

Front view of the eye

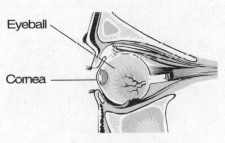

Cross section of the eye

Any injury to the eye is potentially serious and may result in **Impaired vision** or **blindness.** Your quick response and the **correct first aid may help prevent permanent damage to the eye.**

Eye protection

2

Eye protection helps to prevent eye injuries.

At home, at play or at work, you should adopt the following **safety practices**:

◆ wear safety glasses or a face shield when you work with tools or dangerous chemicals

◆ keep chemicals off high shelves and take care to avoid splashes
◆ wear eye protection when you play sports such as squash, racquetball or hockey
◆ wear dark glasses with UV 400 protection or a wide-brimmed hat in sunlight or when light reflects from snow or water

◆ avoid looking into bright lights such as an arc welding flash or an eclipse of the sun

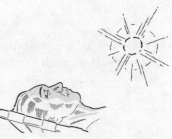

Particles in the eye

3

Particles, such as sand, grit or loose eyelashes, may enter the eye causing pain, redness or watering of the eye.

Never attempt to remove a particle from the eye when:

◆ it is on the cornea

◆ it is adhering to or embedded in the eyeball

◆ the eye is inflamed and painful

Particle on the eyeball

To locate and remove a **loose** particle, you may need **to examine the eye**. Follow these **general rules:**

◆ warn the person not to rub her eyes

◆ wash your hands and put gloves on

◆ stand beside the casualty and steady her head

◆ spread the eyelids apart with your thumb and index finger

◆ shine a light across the eye, not directly into it

◆ look for a shadow of the particle

If the particle on the eyeball **is loose and not on the cornea:**

◆ try to remove it with the **moist corner** of a clean facial tissue or cloth

◆ if pain persists after removal, cover the eye and obtain medical help

Note: If the casualty is wearing contact lenses, let her remove the lens— then continue with first aid.

4

If tears do not wash away a small, loose object, and the particle is causing pain **under the upper lid**:

◆ ask the person to pull the upper lid down over the lower lid. The eyelashes on the lower lid may brush away the particle.

If your first examination does not locate the particle in the eye, you should examine under the eyelids.

To examine under the upper eyelid, you should:

◆ seat the casualty facing a good light

◆ wash your hands and put gloves on, if available

◆ stand beside the casualty

◆ steady the head and ask the casualty to look down

◆ place a cotton-tipped applicator stick at the base of the upper eyelid and gently press the lid backwards, but **don't press** on the eye

◆ grasp the upper eyelashes between the thumb and index finger

◆ draw the lid away from the eye, up and over the applicator stick and roll the applicator back

If the particle is visible:

◆ remove it with the moist corner of a clean facial tissue or cloth

◆ if pain persists after removal, cover the eye and obtain medical help

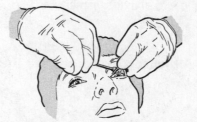 

5

To **look** for a loose particle from **under the lower eyelid,** you should:

- wash your hands and put gloves on
- seat the casualty facing a light
- gently draw the lower eyelid downwards and away from the eyeball while the casualty rolls the eyes upward

If the particle is visible:

- wipe it away with the moist corner of a facial tissue or a clean cloth
- if pain persists after removal, obtain medical help

If a particle does not become visible during your examination and the irritation persists, do not continue your attempts.

- Cover the **injured eye** with an eye pad or gauze and tape loosely in place
- Obtain medical help **immediately**

Covering the injured eye

Note: The reason for **covering the injured eye only** is to reduce psychological stress. If both eyes are injured, cover the eye that is most seriously injured. If both eyes must be covered due to serious injury in both eyes, e.g. intense light burn from arc welding, reassure the casualty often and explain what it is being done and why. A casualty with both eyes covered should be transported on a stretcher.

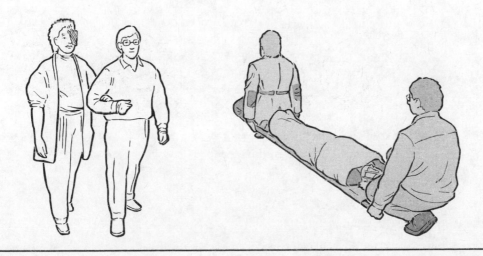

Objects adhering to or embedded in the eye

6

When a **particle** (small object) or a **large object** is stuck to or is embedded in the eye or in the soft tissues near the eye, **do not attempt to remove it.**

You should:

◆ warn the casualty not to rub the eye. It may cause additional pain and irritation

◆ lay the casualty down and support the casualty's head to reduce movement (if available, use a bystander)

◆ wash hands and put on gloves, if available

Depending on the size of the object, use one of the following bandaging techniques.

First aid for a small embedded object or adhered particle:

◆ close the casualty's eyelids and cover the affected eye with a soft eye or gauze pad

◆ extend the covering over the forehead and cheek to avoid pressure on the eye

◆ secure lightly in place with a bandage or adhesive strips

◆ keep the casualty's head immobilized

◆ obtain medical help or transport lying down

◆ give ongoing casualty care until hand over

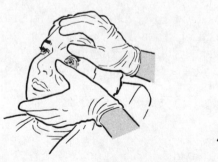  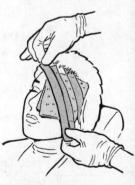

Note: Do not try to remove a contact lens if there has been an injury to the eye other than a chemical burn.

7

First aid for a large embedded object:

◆ lay the casualty down

◆ place dressings around the embedded object, using the "log-cabin technique" (building up dressings around the object) to prevent movement and tape in place

◆ ensure that there is no pressure on the embedded object

◆ immobilize the head to prevent movement

◆ transport the casualty on a stretcher to medical help

◆ give ongoing casualty care until hand over

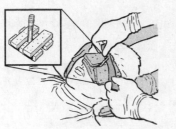
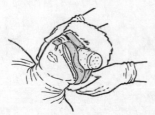

Log-cabin technique

Cup and bandage

Taped cup

Ring pad bandage

Options for stabilizing an embedded object

How to prepare a ring pad

Wounds to the eye

8

A **wound or bruise about the eye** is always serious because there may be underlying damage.

A bruise to the soft tissues around the eye is usually the result of a blow from a blunt object. The bruise may not appear immediately, but there may be damage to the surrounding bones and internal structures. **A wound to the eyeball** from a sharp object is serious because of the possible damage to eyesight. **A wound to the eyelids** may cause **injury to the eyeball**. These wounds usually bleed profusely because of the rich blood supply.

To give first aid for wounds to the eye, you should:

◆ lay the casualty down, supporting the head, to prevent unnecessary movement

◆ wash your hands and put gloves on, if available

◆ close the eyelid and cover the injured eye lightly with a soft eye or gauze pad and tape in place

◆ apply a dressing to the area if there is bleeding. This will usually control it

◆ **never** apply pressure to the eyeball

◆ obtain medical help or transport on a stretcher with the head supported

◆ give ongoing casualty care until hand over

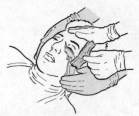
Support the head

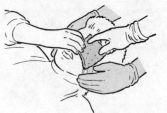
Cover the eye

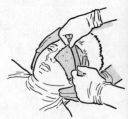
Tape gauze in place

9

From the following statements, select the correct first aid for wounds near the eye. Place a checkmark ☑ in the appropriate boxes.

☐ A. Place the casualty at rest and prevent the head from moving.

☐ B. Heavy bleeding from the eye should be controlled with direct pressure.

☐ C. When bleeding from an eyelid has stopped, leave the dressing in place and bandage the injured eye.

☐ D. You should bandage a bruised eye tightly to stop the internal bleeding.

☐ E. When giving first aid for wounds to the eye, you should avoid pressing on the eyeball.

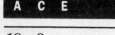

Extruded eyeball

. . . .

10

Severe injury may force the eyeball out of its socket.

Give first aid as follows:

◆   wash hands and put gloves on, if available

◆   **do not try to replace the eye into the socket**

◆   cover the extruded eyeball gently with a moist dressing and a cup and bandage

◆   obtain medical help. If not available,

    ❖   place the casualty face up on a stretcher with the head immobilized for transportation to medical help

    ❖   give ongoing casualty care until hand over

Serious injury could result if the casualty is not kept quiet and moved with great care.

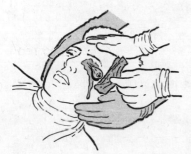 

Moist gauze applied   Cup and bandage

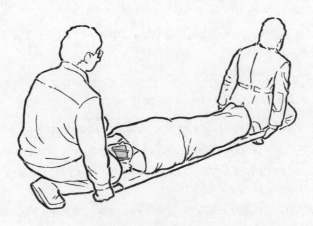

Transport lying down

Burns to the eye

. . . .

11

Eyes can be injured by **corrosive chemicals** (acids or alkalis). Chemical liquids or solids can cause **serious burns.** Casualties usually suffer intense pain.

The aim of first aid is to eliminate and dilute the chemical immediately. **You must act quickly!**

◆   Wash hands and put gloves on, if available

◆   Sit the casualty down with the head tilted back and turned slightly toward the injured side

If the chemical that entered the eye is a **dry powder**, you should first:

◆   brush the chemical away from the eye with a clean, dry cloth. Do **not** use your bare hands

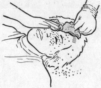

◆   protect the uninjured eye

◆   gently force the casualty's eyelids apart

◆   flush the eye with tepid or cool water for **at least 15 minutes;** flush away from the uninjured eye

◆   cover the injured eye with dressings

◆   when both eyes are affected, cover only the more seriously injured eye, unless the casualty is more comfortable with both eyes covered

◆   get **immediate** medical help

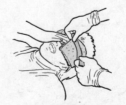

Note: ◆   If the casualty wears contact lenses, ask her to remove them after flushing. If unable to do so, make sure medical help is notified.

◆   Proper eye irrigation equipment should be near at hand when there is a high risk of eye injury from chemicals.

Intense light burns

. . . .

12

Burns to the eyes may be **caused by intense light** such as sunlight reflecting off snow, arc welder's flash or laser beams. Intense light burns **may not be painful at first** but may become very painful several hours after exposure.

When a casualty complains of burning in the eyes after exposure to bright, intense light, you should:

- ◆ wash hands and put gloves on, if available
- ◆ cover both eyes with thick, moist, cool dressings
- ◆ secure them in place (tape or narrow bandage)
- ◆ reassure the casualty as she is temporarily blinded
- ◆ obtain medical help
- ◆ give ongoing casualty care until hand over

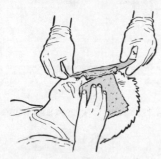

Cover eyes with moist gauze and tape in place

or

Secure moist gauze pads in place with narrow bandages

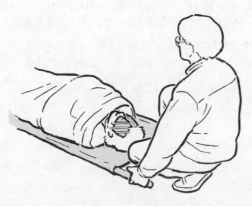

Transport with both eyes covered

Heat burns to the eyelids

12

When a casualty suffers burns to the face from fire, the eyes usually close as a natural reflex to protect the eyes. **Eyelids** may be burned and **need special care.**

First aid for burned eyelids:

◆ wash your hands or put gloves on, if available

◆ cover the eyelids with moist, cool dressings. The casualty will be temporarily blinded, so you must reassure her often and explain what you are doing. If the casualty doesn't want both eyes covered, even after an explanation and reassurance, cover only one eye

◆ secure in place

◆ call for medical help immediately

◆ give ongoing casualty care until hand over

Remember—when there is an injury to an eyelid, there may also be an injury to the eyeball.

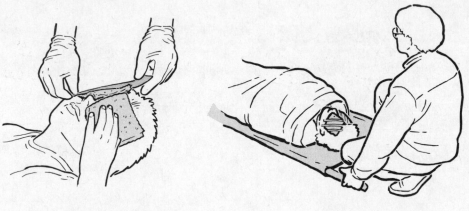

Cover both eyes with moist
gauze

Transport lying down

14

Mark each of the following statements as either true **(T)** or false **(F)**.

☐ A. Burns to the eyelids are not considered serious and don't require medical treatment.

☐ B. Part of the first aid for burned eyelids is to apply several layers of dressings which have been soaked in cool water.

☐ C. Nature protects the eyeballs from heat by cooling them with tears.

☐ D. The application of cool, damp dressings to burned eyelids reduces the skin temperature and relieves pain.

A.F B.T C.F D.T

Eye injuries—review

15

1. A person complains of a dust particle under her upper eyelid. Which of the illustrations below show the correct first aid procedures?
   Check ☑ your answers.

☐ A.

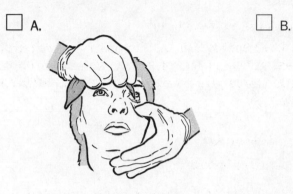

☐ B.

☐ C.

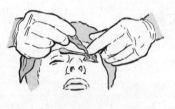

☐ D.

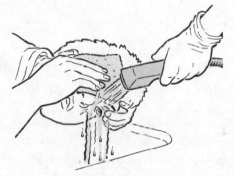

2. If you were unable to remove the particle, which of the following illustrations shows the correct eye covering you should use?
   Check ☑ your answers.

☐ A.

☐ B.

☐ C.

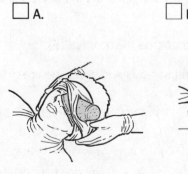

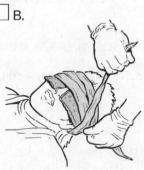

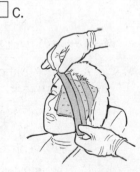

Notes

· ·

EXERCISE 19
BURNS

The skin

1

A basic knowledge of the skin and underlying tissues will help you to understand the serious damage **burns** can do and **to give appropriate first aid.**

Depending on the depth of the burn, the following tissues can be damaged:

◆ top layer of the skin (epidermis)
◆ second layer of the skin (dermis)
◆ fatty tissue
◆ muscle tissue

The skin **protects** the body against injury, extreme temperatures and infection.

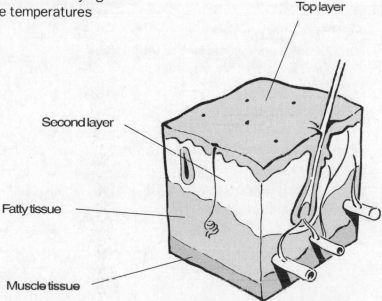

Top layer

Second layer

Fatty tissue

Muscle tissue

Skin and underlying tissues

Prevention of burns

2

Burns are a leading cause of injury in the home, particularly among elderly people and young children. The diagrams below show you **dangerous situations** that may result in a burn.

Prevent burns by paying attention to the symbols shown on labels of hazardous products . . .

Danger corrosive   Danger flammable   Danger explosive   Danger radiation

and by adopting the following **safety measures:**

◆ use hand protection when you touch hot objects or work with corrosive chemicals

◆ keep electric equipment in good repair

◆ store flammable materials in a well-ventilated area

◆ clearly label corrosive and flammable chemicals or radioactive materials and store them in a safe place

◆ do not smoke in bed

◆ supervise children and elderly persons around hot stoves and when bathing

◆ install **smoke alarms and fire extinguishers** in your home and check them as suggested by the manufacturer

◆ develop and practise a fire escape plan

◆ wear protective clothing when exposed to radiation

◆ protect yourself from sunburn by wearing a hat and sunscreen lotion

◆ wear sunglasses when outside in bright light

◆ be cautious around open fires

◆ wear non-flammable clothing

Types of burns

. . . .

3

Burns cause damage to the skin and other underlying tissues.

The types of burns are grouped by their mechanism of injury (cause):

◆ **heat** – dry heat
       – moist heat
       – friction

Dry heat   Moist heat   Friction

◆ **corrosive chemicals**   ◆ **electric current**

◆ **radiation** – ultraviolet rays
           – radioactive materials

U.V. rays   Radioactive materials

Signs and symptoms of burns

4

Signs and symptoms of burns depend on the depth of the burn. The **depth** of a burn is described as the degree of the burn.

First degree burn:

is a superficial burn; only the top layer of the skin is damaged.

You may see:

◆ reddened, dry skin, slight swelling

The casualty may complain of:

◆ pain ranging from mild to severe

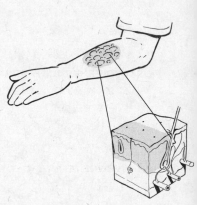

First degree burn

Second degree burn:

is a partial thickness burn; the second layer and the top layer are damaged

You may see:

◆ raw, moist skin, from white to cherry red, blisters with weeping clear fluid

The casualty may complain of:

◆ extreme pain

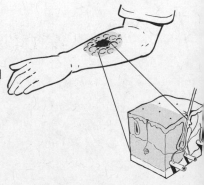

Second degree burn

Third degree burn:

is a deep burn with the full thickness of the skin destroyed; damage may also extend into the underlaying layers of nerves, muscles and fatty tissue. Third degree burns are often accompanied by very painful second degree burns.

You may see:

◆ white, waxy skin, becoming dry and leathery

◆ charred skin and underlaying tissues

The casualty may complain of:

◆ very little or no pain in the deeply burned area

Third degree burn

Seriousness of a burn

5

The seriousness of a burn depends on the:

◆ degree or depth of the burn

◆ amount of body surface burned

This can be determined by the **rule of nines** (dividing the body into multiples of nine) or using the palm of the casulty's hand.. The larger the surface burned, the more serious is the burn.

◆ location of the burn

◆ age of the casualty

Medical help is always required when the burn:

◆ is deep

◆ covers a large area

◆ is located on the face, mouth or throat and can interfere with breathing

◆ is caused by chemicals or an electric current

◆ involves an infant or elderly person

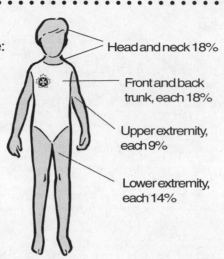

Head and neck 18%

Front and back trunk, each 18%

Upper extremity, each 9%

Lower extremity, each 14%

Child

Head and neck 9%

Front and back trunk, each 18%

Upper extremity, each 9%

Genitalia 1%

Lower extremity, each 18%

the palm = 1%

Severity of burns			
	Percentage of body with burns of the:		
Severity	**3rd degree**	**2nd degree**	**1st degree**
critical burn	>10% (>2% in a child) or any part of the face, hands, feet or genitals	>30% (>20% in a child)	>70%
moderate burn	2–10% face, hands or feet not burned	15–30% (10–20% in a child)	50–70%
minor burn	<2%	<15% (<10% in a child)	<20% face, hands, feet or genitals **not** burned

Smoke inhalation

6

The air passages and the lungs can be seriously damaged by inhaling smoke from a fire. The smoke itself can be **poisonous**.

To reduce the risk of smoke inhalation:

◆ stay close to the ground
◆ cover your mouth and nose with a wet cloth
◆ get out of the area as quickly as possible
◆ in industrial fires, don't enter the fire area without the proper safety equipment

Cover your mouth and nose with a wet cloth

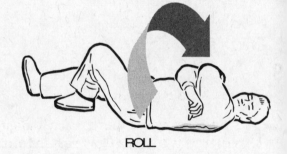

Stay close to the ground

If your clothing catches fire:

◆ **STOP** moving—don't run
◆ **DROP** to the ground
◆ **ROLL** several times to put the flames out

STOP

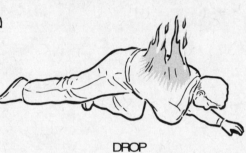

DROP

ROLL

7

You are trying to escape from of a room engulfed in flames. Your jacket has started to burn. Which of the following actions should you take to prevent serious burn damage to yourself?

From the options below, check ☑ the correct answers.

☐ A. Roll on the floor if your clothes are on fire.
☐ B. Get up and run towards the door.
☐ C. Crawl on the floor towards the door.
☐ D. Breath through a moist handkerchief.
☐ E. Open the windows for more fresh air.

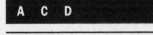

First aid for heat burns

8

When you get burned, **immediately cool the burned area:**

◆ immerse the burned part in **cool water** until pain is relieved

◆ remove jewellery

◆ loosen tight clothing before swelling occurs

If immersing the burned area is not possible, you should:

◆ gently pour cool water over the burned area or

◆ apply a clean cloth soaked in cool water

Immerse in cool water

Cooling a burn will:

◆ **reduce** the temperature of the burned area and prevent further tissue damage

◆ **reduce** swelling and blistering

◆ **relieve** pain

When the pain has lessened:

◆ cover the burned area loosely with a clean, preferably sterile material

◆ secure the dressing, ensuring that the tape does **not** touch the burned area.

◆ obtain medical help

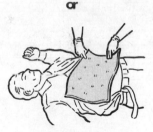

Gently pour cool water over
the burned area

or

9

Check ☑ the correct answer **to each of the following questions**.

You have just burned your hand on a hot stove. Which of the following actions should you do to relieve your pain and avoid more injury to the burned area?

☐ A. Soak your hand in a sink filled with lukewarm water.

☐ B. Cover the burned part with a sterile dressing.

☐ C. Soak your hand in a sink filled with cool water.

☐ D. Take off any rings from your fingers.

A man received a burn to his chest and stomach area. How should you lessen his pain while awaiting medical help?

☐ E. Rinse the affected area with cool, salted water.

☐ F. Apply direct pressure to the burned area.

☐ G. Cover the burn with cool, moist cloths.

☐ H. Apply towels soaked in warm water to the burn.

Cover with wet,
cool cloth

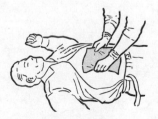

Cover with clean
material

C   D   G

First aid for chemical burns

10

A **corrosive chemical** will continue to burn as long as it is in contact with the skin. To minimize the damage from corrosive chemicals on the skin, **speed is essential**:

- begin scene survey
- **immediately flush the area** with **cool** water
- if necessary, perform a primary survey and give first aid for life-threatening conditions
- flush during removal of clothing
- flush the area **for 15 to 20 minutes**

If the corrosive chemical is a **dry powder**:

- remove contaminated clothing
- brush off any dry powder from the skin
  - ❖ **do not use your bare hands!**
- flush the affected area with cool water **for 15 to 20 minutes**

Following flushing:

- cover the burned area with a clean dressing
- obtain medical help

Note: First aid for specific burns, e.g. from liquid sulphur, may vary from these general rules. You should know the chemicals used in your workplace and the recommended first aid. Check the Workplace Hazardous Materials Information System's (WHMIS) Material Safety Data Sheets (MSDS) available in your workplace.

First aid for electrical burns

11

Burns from an electric current may be more serious than they appear. As well as deep, **third degree** burns at the point of entry and exit, an electric shock can also cause:

- ◆ **stopped breathing**
- ◆ **cardiac arrest**
- ◆ **fractures and dislocations**

To give first aid:

- ◆ begin scene survey
- ◆ shut off the current, **or** get the casualty away from the electrical source, if safe to do so
- ◆ perform primary survey and give life-saving first aid
    - ❖ check for breathing and give AR if needed
    - ❖ check circulation and give CPR if there is no pulse
- ◆ cover the entry and exit wounds with clean dry dressings
- ◆ steady and support fractures and/or dislocations
- ◆ obtain medical help

Electric current

Warning: Never approach a casualty of an electrical injury until the power is turned off. If there are downed wires, call for the power company or other officials to make the scene safe.

Lightning injuries: if someone has been struck by lightning, give first aid for the **apparently dead first**. Casualties of a lightning strike have a greater chance of being revived than a casualty whose heart has stopped because of other causes

Follow these steps

- ◆ Perform a scene survey and make the area safe, e.g. broken trees, glass

    Note: Persons who are struck by lightning are safe to handle. There is no danger of being electrocuted by touching them.

- ◆ Get a brief history and establish the mechanism of injury
- ◆ Steady and support the casualty's head and neck to prevent a possible spinal injury from becoming worse
- ◆ Perform a primary survey
- ◆ Begin CPR to maintain breathing and circulation
- ◆ Once circulation is restored, monitor breathing and pulse continuously. The casualties may arrest again
- ◆ Give ongoing casualty care until hand over to medical help

Shut off the power at the source

First aid for radiation burns

12

There is no specific first aid for radiation burns caused by radioactive materials. Workers involved with radioactive materials should learn the specific procedures and first aid for radioactive exposure. But first aid can be given for a radiation burn caused by the sun.

Minor sunburn

◆ Sponge the burned area with cool water
  or cover the area with a cloth soaked in cool water

◆ Apply sunburn ointment or cream according to the direction on the label

  Caution: Some of these preparations may cause allergic reactions. Sunburn is the only burn to which an ointment is applied.

◆ Protect burned areas from the sun

◆ Do not break blisters

Major sunburn

◆ Give first aid as for heat burns, monitor the casualty for shock

◆ Monitor the casualty for heatstroke

◆ If the casualty vomits or develops a fever get medical help immediately

Minor sunburn

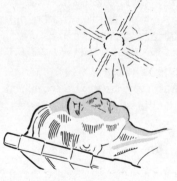

Major sunburn

Radioactive material
burn

Complications that may result from burns

13

A burn may be complicated by:

*   **breathing problems**
    *   ❖ severe burns about the face indicate the casualty may have inhaled hot smoke or fumes
*   **shock**
    *   ❖ caused by loss of body fluids and pain
*   **infection**
    *   ❖ is a serious threat when the skin is burned and underlying tissue is exposed
*   **swelling**
    *   ❖ particularly if jewellery or tight clothing cuts off circulation to the burned area

Infection

Precautions when giving first aid for burns

When giving first aid for a burn, avoid causing further injury and contamination.

*   **DO NOT** overcool the casualty causing a dangerous lowering of body temperature
*   **DO NOT** remove anything sticking to the burn. This may cause further damage and contamination
*   **DO NOT** break blisters
*   **DO NOT** touch the burn with your fingers
*   **DO NOT** breathe, talk or cough over the burn
*   **DO NOT** apply lotions, oils, butter or fat to the injury
*   **DO NOT** cover the burn with cotton wool, adhesive dressings or tape

Take off rings before swelling occurs

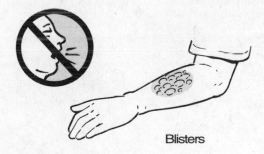

Blisters

14

Mark each statement below that describes how to prevent complications of burns as true **(T)** or false **(F)**.

*   ☐ A. Watch for breathing difficulties of the burned casualty.
*   ☐ B. Watch for signs of pale, cold, clammy skin and a weak, rapid pulse.
*   ☐ C. Remove any rings before the tissue swells.
*   ☐ D. Pull away a casualty's blouse that is clinging to the burned skin.
*   ☐ E. Use your clean fingers to remove pieces of burned skin and clothing.
*   ☐ F. Drain blisters before applying a dressing.

A.T B.T C.T D.F E.F F.F

Notes

· ·

EXERCISE 20

POISONS, BITES AND STINGS

Causes of poisoning

1

Poison

A **poison** is any substance that can cause injury, illness or death when it enters the body.

Poison Symbol

Many common substances can be poisonous and are **not identified** with any danger, warning or caution sign.

Examples of these are:

◆ tobacco

◆ alcohol

◆ some common household and garden plants

◆ contaminated food

◆ medications when taken improperly

Many substances that are not poisonous in small amounts are harmful in large amounts. Look for specific information on product labels.

Some substances are labelled as poisons with signs that you should recognize:

Danger Poison

Prevention of poisoning

2

The best way to deal with poisoning is to prevent it from happening.

Many **poisonings in the home** could be prevented by paying attention to the symbols on the labels of hazardous products and the following safety measures:

◆ Be sure to understand instructions before using medicines, chemicals or insecticides

◆ Keep poisonous substances in their original containers. If not possible, be sure to label with poison symbol

◆ Make sure garages and work areas containing toxic chemicals are well ventilated

◆ Teach children to avoid poisonous indoor and outdoor plants

◆ Prevent errors by carefully checking the **five rights** for giving medication:

❖ **right** medication—read the label carefully

❖ **right** person—medication prescribed for one person should not be taken by another

❖ **right** time—take medication only at the time(s) explained by the doctor

❖ **right** route—take medication only by the method explained by the doctor: swallow by mouth, inhale through nose/mouth; rub into skin, etc.

❖ **right** amount—only take the recommended amount; too much can make people sick; too little will be ineffective

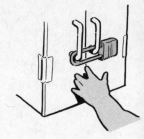

◆ Keep all medications, cleaning products, and other poisonous products out of reach of children

◆ Use child-resistant safety caps on medications and other products, if available

◆ Safely dispose of outdated products by following local regulations

◆ Call your regional **Poison Information Centre** or your doctor for prevention and first aid information about poisoning before going to an isolated area, more than one hour away from a telephone

To prevent **poisoning in the workplace**, employers and employees should follow government guidelines as outlined in the **Workplace Hazardous Materials Information System (WHMIS)**.

3

Each of the pictures below illustrates a dangerous situation/mechanism of injury that could lead to poisoning.

Match each situation with the relating safety measure. Write the appropriate number into the squares provided.

☐ A.

☐ B.

☐ C.

☐ D.

Safety measures

1. Ensure fresh air in rooms where gas fumes are present.
2. Wear proper clothing when you may be in contact with poisonous substances.
3. Keep poisonous substances in original containers.
4. Store poisonous substances, including medication, safely out of the reach of children.

How poisons enter the body

. . . .

4

Poisons can enter the body in **four** different ways.

A poison may be –

◆ **taken by mouth** (ingested), e.g. spoiled food, poisonous liquids, overdose of medication or other substances

◆ **inhaled** through the airway, e.g. exhaust fumes, silo gases, fumes from glues, paint

◆ **absorbed** through the skin, e.g. poisonous house plants, poison ivy, insecticides

◆ **injected** through the skin, e.g. drugs, insect stings

History of a poisoning emergency

5

In any case of suspected poisoning, try to determine the **history of the incident**. There are **four basic facts** you and the Poison Information Centre need to know to give the appropriate first aid.

Ask the conscious casualty, ask bystanders or find out by checking the scene:

◆ **what** kind of poison was taken?
  ❖ look on labels for product names, the ingredient list, and warning symbols
  ❖ smell for distinctive chemical odors
◆ **how** much was taken?
  ❖ estimate amount, if possible, and how easily the product was taken
  ❖ estimate the size/age of the casualty
◆ **how** did the poison enter the body? Swallowed, inhaled, absorbed through the skin, etc?
◆ **when** was the poison taken?

Use your common sense to find out all you can about the poisoning incident.

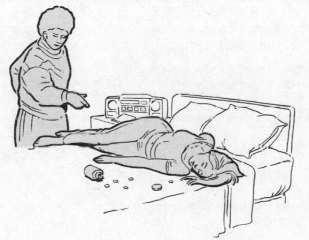

6

You find a 4-year old playing in the garden with an open bottle of liquid pesticide in his hands. What information should you try to find out immediately?

Check ☑ the correct answers.

☐ A. Where did he find the poison?
☐ B. Did he drink the poison?
☐ C. Was the poison in a locked cupboard?
☐ D. What quantity of poison, if any, did he drink?
☐ E. If he drank the poison, how long ago was it?

General first aid for poisoning

7

When you suspect that a person has taken a poison, **act quickly** but do not panic:

◆ begin scene survey

◆ remove person from danger. Be careful not to be harmed yourself from poisons that could be absorbed through the lungs or skin

◆ determine the history of the incident

◆ assess the person's responsiveness

If the person is unconscious:

◆ call medical help immediately

◆ perform a primary survey

◆ if you need to give **artificial respiration** and there is poisonous material around the mouth, use the **mouth-to-nose method** of AR, or use a protective face mask

◆ place the unconscious, breathing person into the recovery position and monitor breathing closely

◆ give ongoing care until medical help takes over

Never try to make an unconscious or drowsy person vomit!

If the person is conscious:

◆ call the **Poison Information Centre** in your region, give them the history (what, how, how much/how old, when) of the incident and **follow their advice on first aid**. You will find the number of the Poison Information Centre at the beginning of the telephone directory, or call directory assistance

Swallowed poisons

The following may indicate that the poison was **taken by mouth** (ingested).

You may note:

◆ a half- or completely empty pill box, cleaning fluid bottle, or other container
◆ discoloured lips, burns in or around the mouth, e.g. from corrosives
◆ smell on the breath, e.g. from the distinctive smells of bleach, gasoline etc.
◆ vomiting, diarrhea
◆ breathing problems and
◆ unconsciousness

The person may complain of:

◆ nausea
◆ abdominal cramps

The signs and symptoms may appear immediately or be delayed.

If the person Is conscious and you cannot immediately reach a Poison Information Centre:

◆ begin scene survey
◆ perform a primary survey and give first aid for life-threatening conditions
◆ wipe the person's face to **remove** any poisonous/corrosive material
◆ **rinse or wipe out** the mouth
◆ **do not dilute** the poison, drinking water or milk may cause more harm
◆ **never induce vomiting** except on advice from the Poison Information Centre
◆ obtain **medical help** quickly
◆ **give ongoing casualty care** until handover to medical help

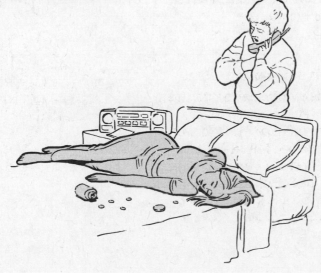

9

When you reach the Poison Information Centre they may tell you to give the conscious casualty **syrup of ipecac** to induce vomiting.

You may also be told **not** to make a person vomit who has swallowed a:

◆ a medication that inhibits vomiting, or which is rapid acting

◆ corrosive product, such as a drain cleaner; it will burn again when vomited

◆ petroleum-based product, such as kerosene; the vomit may enter the lungs and cause severe breathing problems

◆ unconscious casualties should never be made to vomit

Syrup of ipecac can be bought in single-dose bottles (14ml) at most drug stores without prescription.

One bottle for every child under ten years of age should be kept in a locked medicine cabinet and should be given only under direction of the **Poison Information Centre.**

The **expiry date** on the bottles should be **checked** regularly and the bottles replaced if necessary.

If the contents freeze or reach a temperature above 30° C. do not use -discard and replace it.

In remote areas without easy access to a pharmacy you must be prepared for an emergency. Know how to contact your nearest Poison Information Centre, and be pepared to follow their instructions.

10

Mark each of the following statements as either true **(T)** or false **(F)**.

☐ A. If the person has swallowed a corrosive or oil-based chemical, you should immediately make the person vomit.

☐ B. A doctor's prescription is necessary for buying syrup of ipecac.

☐ C. Vomit containing petroleum can harm the airway.

☐ D. Making someone gag always causes vomiting.

☐ E. Syrup of ipecac has an expiry date.

nhaled poisons

1

The following may indicate that a poison was inhaled:

You may observe:

◆ strange odours, fumes or smoke at the scene

◆ breathing problems

◆ coughing

◆ unconsciousness

The person may complain of:

◆ headache

◆ dizziness

◆ chest pain

Inhaled poisons, such as glue and gas fumes should b
cleared from the lungs as quickly as possible.

You should:

◆ begin scene survey. If the area is unsafe, do not enter. In a closed space, open
a door for fresh air. Call for assistance from neighbours or friends

◆ **remove** the person from the source of gas or vapour to fresh air

❖ if the casualty is unresponsive, turn into the recovery position, and call
medical help immediately

◆ perform a primary survey, and give first aid for life-threatening conditions

◆ monitor breathing closely

◆ obtain medical help as quickly as possible

◆ give **ongoing care** until hand over to medical help

12

You find an unresponsive person in a small room. The scene survey suggests that
he has inhaled gas fumes from a stove. You send for medical help. Which of the
following should you do?

Check ☑ the correct answers.

☐ A. Remove the stove with the gas leak.

☐ B. Drag the person outside.

☐ C. Check for breathing.

☐ D. Begin artificial respiration if breathing stops.

B C D

Absorbed poisons

13

The following may indicate that a poison has been **absorbed** through the skin:

You may see:

- ◆ poisonous plants, spilled insecticide, crop-spraying
- ◆ reddened skin, blisters, swelling or severe burns
- ◆ breathing problems
- ◆ unconsciousness

The person may complain of:

- ◆ itching or burning of affected skin
- ◆ headache, dizziness
- ◆ nausea

Poisons that may be absorbed **must be removed from the skin as quickly as possible.**

You should:

- ◆ begin scene survey
- ◆ perform a primary survey, and give first aid for life-threatening conditions
- ◆ **flush** the affected area with **large amounts of cool water**
  - ❖ if the poisonous substance is a powder, brush off excessive amounts with a dry cloth **before** flushing
- ◆ **wash** the skin with soap and water, if possible
  - ❖ pay careful attention to hidden areas, e.g. under the fingernails, in the hair
- ◆ monitor breathing closely
- ◆ obtain medical help as soon as possible
- ◆ give ongoing care until hand over to medical help

Injected poisons

14

When a poison has been injected through the skin:

You may see:

◆ disposable needles, injectable drugs, bee stings, etc. at the scene
◆ irritation at the site of injection
◆ breathing problems
◆ changes in pulse rates
◆ unconsciousness

The person may complain of:

◆ headache
◆ dizziness
◆ nausea

To reduce the spread of an injected poison throughout the body:

You should:

◆ begin scene survey
◆ perform primary survey, and give first aid for life-threatening conditions
◆ keep the person **at rest**
◆ keep the limb with the injection site, or bite site, **below heart level**
◆ monitor breathing closely
◆ obtain medical help as quickly as possible
◆ give ongoing care until hand over to medical help

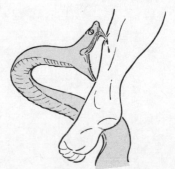

Animal/human bites

15

Animal and human bites that break the skin may cause serious infection.

If you suspect that the bite was caused by an animal infected with **rabies, act quickly** and obtain **medical help urgently.** The infection can be prevented by immediate immunization.

Protect yourself:

◆ wear protective gloves, if available, when giving first aid and when you must handle the infected animal

◆ scrub your hands thoroughly after these procedures

To give first aid:

◆ **allow moderate bleeding** to cleanse the wound

◆ control bleeding if it is severe

◆ **wash** the wound with an antiseptic soap or detergent and water

◆ apply a dressing and bandage

◆ obtain medical help as soon as possible

Because of infectious diseases (e.g. rabies) each animal/human bite that breaks the skin should be checked by medical help.

16

Which of the following statements are correct when dealing with an animal/human bite?

Check your answers.

☐ A. Allow some bleeding to help clean the wound.

☐ B. Use cold water to kill the germs in the wound.

☐ C. Rabies is a potentially deadly disease.

☐ D. You can help to avoid a serious infectious disease following an animal bite by getting medical help without delay.

☐ E. It is not necessary to identify the attacking animal to find out if it has been vaccinated against rabies.

Snakebite

17

You may identify a poisonous snakebite by the following signs and symptoms:

You may see:

- two tiny holes in the skin
- swelling and discolouration
- chills and sweating
- vomiting
- breathing difficulty

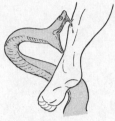

Snakebite

The person may complain of:

- burning in the area of the bite, followed by
- severe pain about the wound
- chills
- nausea
- general weakness

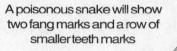

A poisonous snake will show
two fang marks and a row of
smaller teeth marks

First aid is required urgently:

- begin scene survey—look for clues, call for help, etc.
- perform a primary survey, and give first aid for life-threatening conditions
- calm and reassure the casualty
- **place** the casualty **at rest** in a semisitting position
- steady and support the affected limb and keep it **below heart level**
- **flush** the bite area with soapy water, if available
- **immobilize** the limb as for a fracture and transport the person to **medical help immediately**
- monitor breathing closely

Precautions in giving first aid for a snakebite:

- make sure there is no further danger from the snake
- **do not apply ice** to the wound, this could cause more damage
- **do not let the person walk** if there is any other transportation to medical help
- **do not give the person alcoholic** beverages
- **do not try to suck the poison** out of the wound with your mouth **or cut the bite mark with a knife**
- if the snake is killed, bring it to medical help for identification

Warning!

Insect bites and stings

18

Bee sting

In most persons, an insect bite or sting causes only some painful swelling with redness and itching. **Bee and wasp stings**, however, may cause **severe allergic reactions** in some people.

Allergic reactions are recognized by the following –

You may see:

◆ hives and swelling especially on the face

◆ vomiting

◆ breathing difficulty

◆ loss of consciousness

The person may complain of:

◆ nausea

◆ breathing difficulty

◆ sense of impending doom

When these signs occur, **obtain medical help urgently.**

While awaiting medical help **give first aid as follows:**

◆ **assist** the person to take prescribed medication if available

◆ If an **EpiPen® Auto-Injector** or **AnaKit®** are available, follow the casualty's instructions, or the instruction on the labels

◆ keep the limb below heart level

◆ monitor breathing

EpiPen® Auto-Injector

Ana-Kit®

19

To give **first aid** to the site of the bite or sting:

◆ **scrape** the stinger and poison sac carefully from the skin, if it is still present, with the blunt edge of a knife or credit card. Do not squeeze the stinger while removing it.

◆ **apply** rubbing alcohol, or a paste of baking soda and water

◆ if the sting is in the mouth, give the person a **mouthwash** of one teaspoon of baking soda to a glass of water, or **ice** to suck

◆ if there is swelling in the mouth, and breathing difficulties, get immediate medical help. Monitor the person closely

Scraping stinger with knife

Bee sting

Applying paste of baking soda and water

20

Mark each of the following statements as either true **(T)** or false **(F)**.

☐ A. Discomfort and a stinging sensation are normal reactions to an insect bite.

☐ B. Baking soda mixed with water will soothe a sting.

☐ C. The stinger should be left in the skin to prevent further injury.

☐ D. The application of heat may help to reduce pain and swelling in the mouth.

A.T   B.T   C.F   D.F

Leeches and ticks

. . . .

21

Leeches (bloodsuckers) are found in swamps, ponds and stagnant water. They attach themselves to the human body by making a tiny hole in the skin. Forceful removal of leeches may cause injury to the skin and infection.

First aid for leech bites:

◆ **remove** the leech by applying salt, a lighted match (be careful!) turpentine or c to its body

◆ **do not pull** or **scrape** it off the skin

◆ **wash** the area around the bite

◆ **apply** a weak solution of baking soda or ammonia to relieve irritation

Ticks are found in forests and drop from leaves onto animals and humans. They bite through the skin and attach themselves. **Infection** from ticks may be harmful

First aid for tick bites:

◆ wear protective gloves, if available

◆ **grasp** the tick with tweezers as close to the casualty's skin as possible

◆ **pull** the tick away from the skin with an **even steady pull**

◆ avoid squashing a tick during removal; infected blood may spurt on you

◆ **clean** the area around the bite with soap and water

◆ wash your hands

◆ **keep the tick for identification**

◆ **obtain** medical help if the bite becomes infected

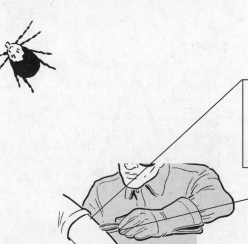

tweezers
removing tick

Wear protective gear when removing ticks

MEDICAL CONDITIONS
(DIABETES, CONVULSIONS, ASTHMA & ALLERGIES)

Diabetic emergencies

1

The body needs **energy** to function. The energy comes from sugar that the body gets from the food you eat.

Diabetes is a condition in which the body cannot convert sugar into energy because of **a lack of insulin**.

Insulin is a substance produced by the body to regulate the use of sugar. Normally there is a balance between the sugar used and the insulin produced.

A **diabetic emergency** occurs when there is a severe imbalance between the amount of insulin and sugar in the body.

Normal balance between insulin and sugar

2

Causes of diabetic emergencies

Diabetes is a condition in which the body does **not produce enough insulin,** causing the sugar level to be out of balance.

To balance the sugar level, a person with diabetes may take prescribed amounts of the medication, either by mouth or by injection.

Two conditions may result in a diabetic emergency:

Diabetic Coma

Not enough insulin, causing a high level of sugar—diabetic coma (also called hyperglycemia)

Insulin Shock

Too much insulin, causing a low level of sugar—insulin shock (also called hypoglycemia)

Insulin

Sugar

Insulin

Sugar

May be caused by:

◆   not taking enough insulin

◆   eating too much food/alcohol

◆   doing less exercise than usual

May be caused by:

◆   taking too much insulin

◆   not eating enough food or vomiting

◆   doing more exercise than usual

How to recognize a diabetic emergency

3

A **conscious casualty with diabetes** might be able to tell you what is wrong. However, keep in mind that the person may be confused.

An **unconscious casualty** may be wearing a **medical alert** bracelet or necklace that will tell you that she has diabetes.

If the casualty cannot tell you what she needs, look for the following signs and symptoms:

Do you know what is wrong?

	Insulin shock (needs sugar)	**Diabetic coma** (needs insulin)
Time to develop	Develops very rapidly	Develops over hours or days
Pulse:	strong and rapid	weak and rapid
Breathing:	shallow	deep and sighing
Skin:	pale and sweating	flushed, dry and warm
Breath odour:	odourless	like musty apple or nail polish
LOC:	faintness to unconsciousness developing quickly	gradual onset of unconsciousness
Other signs and symptoms	headache trembling hunger	unsteady walk nausea

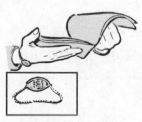

Medical alert devices

Warning

Don't confuse a diabetic emergency with alcoholic intoxication. Many of the behavioural signs are the same, but a person having a diabetic emergency needs immediate medical help. Check the signs and look for a medical alert device.

First aid for a diabetic emergency

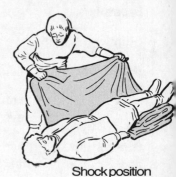

4

The first aid for insulin shock and diabetic coma is the same:

◆ begin scene survey

  ❖ if the casualty is **unresponsive**, get medical help immediately

◆ do a primary survey and give first aid for life-threatening conditions

◆ place the unconscious person into the recovery position and monitor the ABCs until medical help takes over

◆ look for a medical alert device that will give you more information about the casualty's condition

If the **casualty** is **conscious** and knows what is wrong:

◆ assist her to take what is needed—**sugar or her prescribed medication**

If the casualty is **confused** about what is required:

◆ give her something sweet to eat or drink and get medical help, sugar will quickly relieve **insulin shock**, but will not worsen **diabetic coma**

Unresponsive casualty

Give something sweet

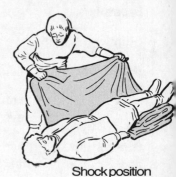
Shock position

5

Which of the following actions should you take when a diabetic emergency occurs?

Check ☑ the correct answers.

☐ A. Give a conscious diabetic person several glasses of cool water to drink.

☐ B. Give a conscious casualty candy or orange juice if she is not sure what she needs.

☐ C. Send someone to telephone for medical help if the sweetened drink does not improve the casualty's condition.

☐ D. Place an unconscious diabetic person in the best position to ensure an open airway.

☐ E. Help a conscious casualty to take her medication if she says she needs it and asks for your assistance.

How to recognize an epileptic seizure

6

Epilepsy is a disorder of the nervous system. It may result in recurring convulsions, called **epileptic seizures,** involving partial or complete loss of consciousness. In most cases epilepsy is controlled by medication and seizures don't happen often. An **epileptic seizure** may come on **suddenly** and **is usually very brief.**

Any of the following signs and symptoms will help you to identify a major epileptic seizure–

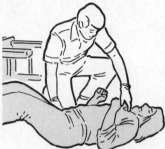

You may see:

◆ the casualty falling to the floor

◆ sudden loss of consciousness

◆ noisy breathing, through clenched teeth

◆ frothing at the mouth, if he produces lots of saliva

◆ grinding of teeth

◆ convulsions (uncontrollable muscle contractions) with arching of the back

◆ the casualty may lose control over bladder and bowel functions

Convulsions

Some casualties may complain of:

◆ a sensation such as a sound, smell or feeling of movement in the body that tells them that a seizure is about to occur. This is called an **aura**.

On regaining consciousness the person may be unaware of recent events and be confused and very tired.

Aura

First aid for an epileptic seizure

7

The **aim of first aid** for an epileptic seizure is to protect the casualty from injury during the period of convulsions.

You should:

◆ begin scene survey

◆ clear the area of hard or sharp objects that could cause injury

◆ clear the area of onlookers to **ensure privacy** for the casualty

◆ **guide** but **do not restrict** movement

◆ carefuly loosen tight clothing

◆ turn the casualty gently to the side with her face turned slightly downward. This will allow for drainage and prevent her tongue from falling back into her throat

◆ **do not** attempt to force the casualty's mouth open or to put anything between her teeth

When convulsions have stopped:

◆ place her into the recovery position and wipe away any fluids from the mouth and nose

◆ do a secondary survey to see if the casualty was injured during the seizure

◆ give ongoing casualty care, monitor breathing and allow her to rest

The casualty usually recovers quickly. If you know the convulsions were caused by epilepsy, you do not need to call medical help.

Call for medical help:

◆ if a second seizure occurs within minutes

◆ if the casualty is unconscious for more than five minutes

◆ if it is the person's first seizure or the cause is unknown

◆ if serious injuries have resulted

Make area safe

Place casualty onto side to allow for drainage

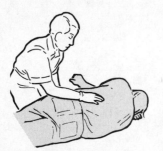

Recovery position

8

A woman in a crowded store suddenly falls to the floor and goes into convulsions. What should you do?

Check ☑ the correct answers.

☐ A. Tell the bystanders to form a circle around the woman.

☐ B. Clear away all objects on which she could hurt herself.

☐ C. Hold her arms firmly to prevent injury.

☐ D. Watch her closely to ensure she is breathing.

☐ E. Position her to maintain an open airway.

B D E

Convulsions in children

An infant or young child with a **rapid rise in body temperature** to 40°C or 104°F is at risk of convulsions. A fever emergency is when the temperature taken in the armpit is 38°C (100.5°F) or higher for an infant and 40°C (104°F) or higher for a child.

First aid for fever may prevent the onset of convulsions
Advise the parent/caregiver to:
◆ call the doctor immediately and follow her advice
◆ give acetaminophen (e.g. Tempra® or Tylenol® according to directions on the label) if the doctor can't be reached
◆ **not give ASA** (e.g. Aspirin®), it may cause Reye's syndrome, a life-threatening condition, in children and adolescents
◆ encourage the child to drink fluids
◆ sponge the child with lukewarm water for about 20 minutes if the temperature doesn't go down. Don't immerse the child in a tub
◆ monitor the child's temperature and repeat these steps if necessary

Remove clothing

Sponge with tepid water

Fever convulsions can be recognized by the same signs as an epileptic seizure *(see page 21–5).*
First aid for fever convulsions is to:
◆ protect the child from injury. Clear the area of hard or sharp objects that could cause injury
◆ loosen constrictive clothing
◆ not restrain the child
When convulsions cease:
◆ place the child into the best recovery position for his age, with the head lowered and turned to one side
◆ reassure the child's parents
◆ obtain medical help

Asthma

. . . .

10

Bronchial asthma, often simply called, **asthma,** involves repeated attacks of shortness of breath with wheezing and coughing.

Asthma causes narrowing of the airways in the lungs which is due to:

◆ tightening of the muscles in the airways

◆ swelling of the inner lining of the airway (bronchi and bronchioles)

◆ an increase in the amount and thickness of the mucus

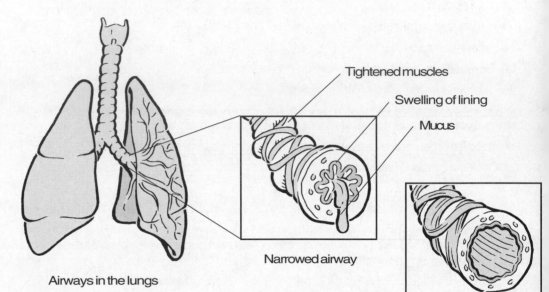

Tightened muscles

Swelling of lining

Mucus

Narrowed airway

Airways in the lungs

Healthy airway

. . . .

11

Check ☑ the statements below which correctly explain why the airways narrow.

☐ A. The lining of the airways becomes thicker.

☐ B. The mucus becomes thinner and more scanty.

☐ C. The muscles in the walls of the airways contract.

☐ D. More mucus develops and it becomes stickier.

Causes of an acute asthmatic attack

. . . .

12

Asthmatic attacks are usually caused by exposure to certain **triggers.** These triggers vary widely among people with asthma.

Common triggers include, e.g.:

◆ house dust
◆ smoke
◆ pollen
◆ insects
◆ furry or feathered animals, e.g. dogs, cats, birds
◆ certain foods
◆ certain drugs
◆ a cold
◆ stress/emotional upsets

Although asthmatic attacks can be triggered unexpectedly, preventive measures can be taken by avoiding triggers known to cause an attack.

Triggers for allergic reaction/asthma

How to recognize a severe asthmatic attack

13

Asthmatic attacks vary in how rapidly they begin, how severe they are and how long they last. A **mild** asthmatic attack can be annoying. A **severe** asthmatic attack can be fatal.

You can recognize a **severe asthmatic attack** by the following signs and symptoms:

- shortness of breath with obvious trouble breathing
- coughing or wheezing (a whistling noise when air moves through the narrowed airways) may get louder or stop
- fast and shallow breathing
- tightness in the chest
- casualty sitting upright trying to breathe, in the tripod position
- bluish colour in the face
- fast pulse rate
- anxiety
- restlessness, then fatigue
- shock

Tripod Position

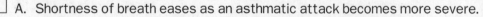

14

Mark each of the following statements as either true **(T)** or false **(F)**.

☐ A. Shortness of breath eases as an asthmatic attack becomes more severe.

☐ B. All people with asthma wheeze during a severe asthmatic attack.

☐ C. Wheezing is the sound of air in smaller than normal airways.

☐ D. If a person with asthma is anxious, has sweaty, bluish/grey skin, is sitting and has difficulty with each breath, the attack is severe.

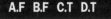
A.F B.F C.T D.T

First aid for a severe asthmatic attack

15

If the casualty shows increasing breathing difficulties:

You should:

◆ call for medical help immediately

◆ have the casualty stop any activity

◆ place the casualty in the most comfortable position for breathing. This is usually sitting upright, leaning slightly forward and resting on a support

◆ provide reassurance because fear will increase the breathing rate

◆ do not encourage drinking during an attack. Fluids may get into the lungs

◆ assist the casualty to take her prescribed medication if you are asked to do so (see next page)

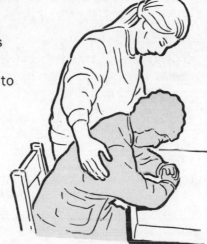

Position casualty

16

A middle aged man shows signs of a severe asthmatic attack with more and more trouble breathing. To help him, which choice of action should you take?

Check ☑ your choices.

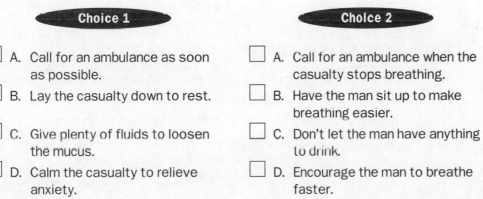

Choice 1

☐ A. Call for an ambulance as soon as possible.

☐ B. Lay the casualty down to rest.

☐ C. Give plenty of fluids to loosen the mucus.

☐ D. Calm the casualty to relieve anxiety.

Choice 2

☐ A. Call for an ambulance when the casualty stops breathing.

☐ B. Have the man sit up to make breathing easier.

☐ C. Don't let the man have anything to drink.

☐ D. Encourage the man to breathe faster.

A.1 B.2 C.2 D.1

Assisting with inhalers

. . . .

17

The casualty may be too weak or is breathing too rapidly to use the inhaler herself.
You can assist the casualty to take her prescribed medication as follows:

◆ ask the casualty if she requires **your assistance** and which medication is to
   be used

◆ ask for a nod as an answer to your questions to save the casualty from speaking

◆ ask if the container needs to be shaken and assist if needed

◆ remove the cap and hand the inhaler to the casualty for her to use

   ❖ it is not unusual for an asthmatic to take many puffs, if they are having
      difficulty inhaling deeply, or coordinating inhalation and the release of
      medication

◆ if assisting with inhalers is not possible, monitor breathing closely

◆ provide ongoing casualty care until medical help takes over

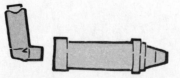

Shake inhaler

A spacer, or aerochamber can hold the medication so the casualty can inhale it
more effectively over several breaths. This is especially important for children.

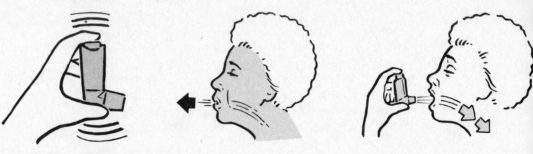

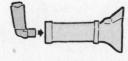

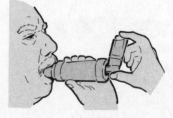

Allergic reactions

. . . .

18

An **allergic reaction** is the response of a body with an abnormal sensitivity to substances that are normally harmless.

Substances causing allergic reactions **enter the body by**:

◆ swallowing (e.g. foods, medications)
◆ inhaling (e.g. dust, pollen)
◆ absorption through the skin (e.g. plants, chemicals)
◆ injection (bee/wasp stings, drugs)

The severity of an allergic reaction varies from minor discomfort to a **severe life-threatening type of shock** (anaphylactic shock).

Triggers

You can recognize a severe allergic reaction by any of the following:

You may see:

◆ sneezing, coughing and red watery eyes
◆ swelling of the face, mouth and throat
◆ laboured breathing with wheezing due to swollen tissues obstructing the airway
◆ a weak, rapid pulse
◆ vomiting and diarrhea
◆ pale skin, blueness or both
◆ changes in level of consciousness

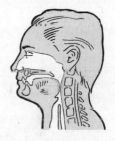

Inflamed airway passages

The casualty may complain of:

◆ tightness in the chest
◆ severe itching with hives (raised skin eruptions)
◆ dizziness
◆ abdominal cramps with nausea

An asthmatic attack is an allergic reaction that results in breathing problems.

First aid for severe allergic reactions

19

EpiPen® Auto-Injector

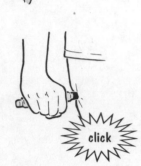

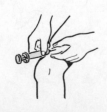

click

A person who has a known, severe allergy, usually carries this information on him:

Medical alert
necklace

Medical alert bracelet

Ana-Kit®

Give **first aid** as follows:

◆ send for medical help

◆ monitor airway, breathing, circulation (ABC's)

◆ maintain breathing and circulation

◆ check for medical alert information

◆ assist the conscious casualty to take prescribed medication, e.g. Ana-Kit® or EpiPen® Auto Injector. Follow the casualty's instructions and the manufacturer's directions. The medication will begin to wear off within 10 to 20 minutes

◆ provide care for shock until medical help takes over

Watch the casualty carefully. An allergic reaction can become life-threatening.

20

Check ☑ the procedures you would follow to give first aid to a person who is having a severe allergic reaction.

☐ A. Call for medical assistance immediately when you note signs of shock.

☐ B. If the casualty has an allergy kit, take him and the kit to a doctor.

☐ C. Ensure adequate breathing and provide artificial respiration if required.

☐ D. Monitor the person's condition continuously until medical personnel takes over or the person has fully recovered.

A C D

Medical conditions—review

21

1. You have a casualty who has asthma and is wheezing noisily. Which illustration below shows the best position for this condition? Check ☑ the correct answer.

☐ A.

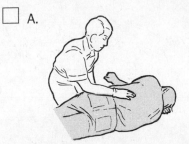

☐ B.

2. Which two illustrations below show the correct first aid for a diabetic casualty who has not eaten for a long time and is feeling sick? Check ☑ the correct answers.

☐ A. Help with an inhaler.

☐ B. Give something sweet.

☐ C. Turn into the recovery position.

☐ D. Call for medical help.

☐ E. Help with an allergy injection.

Notes

· ·

ENVIRONMENTAL INJURIES & ILLNESSES

Temperature regulation

1

The human body normally maintains a temperature of about **37°C** (98.6°F).
A healthy body can adjust to environmental changes and maintain its normal
temperature by:

- ◆ **shivering** which helps produce and retain body heat when it is cold
- ◆ **sweating** which helps to cool the body when it is hot

Temperature
regulation

However, when a person is exposed to extreme cold or extreme hot temperatures,
the temperature control mechanism may break down causing **cold injuries** or **heat
illnesses.** People in poor health, the elderly and young children are particularly
vulnerable.

Cold injuries

2

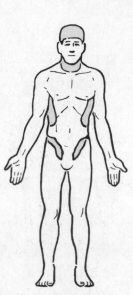

Areas of greatest heat loss

Anywhere in the world where there are cold temperatures people can die from cold exposure. Exposure to extreme cold may cause:

◆ **frostbite** – a local tissue damage

◆ **hypothermia** – a generalized cooling of the body

The **risk of frostbite or hypothermia is increased** when:

◆ low temperature is combined with strong winds. This is called windchill.

◆ the person is elderly, in poor health, or very young

◆ the person is in a weakened condition because of:
   ❖ lack of food
   ❖ fatigue
   ❖ use of alcohol, tobacco or drugs

◆ clothing is wet (from sweating or immersion in water)

◆ clothing does not retain your body heat, e.g. cotton

◆ exposure to the cold is for a long period of time

3

How to prevent cold injuries:

◆ **prepare for the worst conditions**

– take extra clothing when outside in cold weather

◆ **stay warm** – wear several layers of loose fitting clothing that breathes, preferably wool. Silk, polypropylene and polyester pile are best next to the skin

– wear windproof clothing or stay out of the wind

– keep the head and neck covered

◆ **stay dry** – avoid getting wet, even by sweating

◆ **eat well** – eat high energy foods often at regular intervals

◆ **drink lots** – hot, sweet drinks are best, but cold water is fine if nothing else is available

◆ **stay safe** – limit the time spent in the cold

– stay with a partner so you can check each other for signs of cold injury

◆ **avoid fatigue** – rest periodically in sheltered areas

◆ **avoid use of alcohol and/or tobacco**

– these add to heat loss

Properly dressed for the cold—wear multiple layers

4

Listed below are dangerous situations that could result in cold injuries. Match each situation with a safety measure that could prevent the injury. Write the appropriate number in the boxes provided.

Situations

☐ A. Nothing to eat

☐ B. Weakened condition

☐ C. Poor clothing

☐ D. Wet clothing

☐ E. Long exposure

☐ F. No partner

Safety measures

1. Wear warm clothing and protect your head, hands and feet.

2. Carry an extra pair of woollen socks so you can keep your feet dry.

3. Use a "buddy system" to ensure safety.

4. Beware of becoming overtired and don't take alcoholic drinks.

5. Eat foods such as chocolate, nuts or raisins frequently.

6. Stay outside for only short periods when it is very cold.

A.5 B.4 C.1 D.2 E.6 F.3

Stages of frostbite

5

Frostbite is a localized cooling of the body. It may be:

◆ **superficial** – affects the entire thickness of the skin

◆ **deep** – affects the skin and underlying tissues

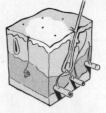

Superficial frostbite

Superficial frostbite usually affects ears, face, fingers and toes.

You may see:

◆ white, waxy skin

◆ skin that is firm to the touch, but the tissues underneath are soft

The casualty may complain of:

◆ pain in early stages followed by numbness in the affected area

Superficial frostbite may progress to **deep frostbite.**

Superficial frostbite

Deep frostbite

Deep frostbite is far more serious. It usually involves an entire hand or foot and affects the tissues beneath the outer layer of the skin. It may be recognized by the following:

You may see:

◆ white, waxy skin that turns greyish blue as frostbite progresses

◆ skin that feels cold and hard

The casualty may complain of:

◆ lack of feeling in the affected area

Lack of feeling

6

Frozen state

A frozen state of the casualty should be suspected when:

◆ the casualty is found in a cold location and is unresponsive

◆ the joints of the jaw and neck appear to be rigid when trying to open the airway

◆ the skin and deeper tissues are cold and cannot be depressed

◆ the entire body moves as a solid unit

Casualty is unresponsive

7

Indicate whether the person described below may have superficial or deep frostbite or is in a frozen state. Place the appropriate number (1, 2, 3) in the boxes provided.

Superficial frostbite (1), deep frostbite (2); frozen state (3)

☐ A. A spot on the cheek is pale and does not feel as soft as the rest of the cheek.

☐ B. A foot is pale and greyish looking. The casualty says that he cannot feel the foot when he places it on the ground.

☐ C. A casualty is found in a snowbank. He does not respond when touched and the body feels hard and icy cold.

☐ D. One ear is white and the casualty complains of a dull feeling in the ear lobe.

☐ E. The tips of the fingers of one hand are colourless and cold. The surface of the skin feels firm but you can feel soft tissue underneath.

☐ F. The casualty says he does not feel it when you touch his hand. The skin feels cold, very firm and looks waxy.

☐ G. When you try to open the airway of an unresponsive casualty, the neck is stiff and the hard, cold flesh cannot be depressed.

A.1 B.2 C.3 D.1 E.1 F.2 G.3

8

First aid for superficial frostbite

- Prevent further heat loss
- **Rewarm** the frost-bitten part **gradually** with the heat of your body by e.g.:
  - ❖ firm steady pressure of a warm hand
  - ❖ breathing on the frost-bitten part
  - ❖ placing the frost-bitten area in close contact with your own body
- **Do not** apply direct heat
- **Do not rub, or put snow** on a frost-bitten area

First aid for deep frostbite

A casualty with deep frostbite requires medical attention.

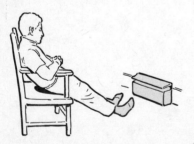

Rewarming with body heat

- **Treat the frozen part gently to prevent further tissue damage**
- Prevent further heat loss
- **Do not rub the limbs.** Do not allow the casualty to move unnecessarily
- **Do not thaw** the frozen part
- Obtain medical help
- Transport by stretcher if lower limbs are affected

Indirect heat

If the casualty must walk –

- do not thaw the frozen limb (walking on a frozen foot is not likely to cause more serious damage)
- help the casualty to make walking easier

Thawing of a frozen body part should only be attempted when –

◆ medical help is not available

◆ the casualty is in a warm environment

◆ there is no danger of refreezing

If thawing of a frozen part is necessary:

◆ provide a warm, comfortable environment

◆ remove clothing gently from the affected part

◆ rewarm the frozen area in warm water at a temperature of about 40°C (104°F) until colour no longer improves. Warmer water will cause extreme pain

◆ carefully dry the affected part

◆ apply sterile dressings loosely on wounds and put sterile pads between toes and fingers

◆ give ongoing casualty care

◆ transport casualty lying down with legs slightly elevated

Rewarming

If a body is found in a frozen state:

◆ do not start CPR, if you are certain that a frozen state exists

◆ call for medical help, so that rewarming may take place under controlled conditions.

Hypothermia

10

Stages of hypothermia

Hypothermia is a generalized cooling of the body, with body temperature falling below 35°C (95°F). It usually develops from exposure to abnormally low temperatures over a prolonged period of time. However, it can also develop in temperatures well above freezing. Watch for early signs of hypothermia and prevent it from becoming worse.

Immersion hypothermia refers to hypothermia caused by being in cold water. A person loses heat 25–30 times faster in water than in air of the same temperature. Immersion hypothermia can happen very quickly, within minutes, if a person falls into cold water. Suspect hypothermia whenever someone falls into water by mistake even in the summer. Immersion hypothermia can also happen more slowly, for instance while swimming or scuba diving in a lake. In these cases, hypothermia creeps up on the casualty, and may not be suspected right away.

The "heat escape lessening position" (HELP)

Sometimes hypothermia is mistaken for other conditions. Hypothermia has been mistaken for drunkenness, stroke and drug abuse. This often happens in the city, where a warm environment doesn't seem far away. For example, an elderly person's home may not feel cold to you since you are warmly dressed, but in fact the room temperature is 15° C, the elderly person is underdressed, and is hypothermic.

Hypothermia may progress from **mild** to **moderate** to **severe** if it is not recognized and first aid is not given immediately.

You may see the following changes in the signs as the casualty's condition becomes more severe.

Signs	Progressive stages of hypothermia		
	Mild	**Moderate**	**Severe**
Pulse	normal	slow and weak	weak, irregular or absent
Breathing	normal	slow and shallow	slow or absent
Appearance	shivering, slurred speech	shivering is violent or stopped, is clumsy and stumbles	shivering has stopped
Mental state	conscious, withdrawn	confused, sleepy, irrational	unconscious

First aid for hypothermia

11

The **aims of first aid for hypothermia** are to:

◆ prevent further loss of body heat

◆ obtain medical help as quickly as possible

When a casualty is suffering from hypothermia, you should:

◆ **handle him gently** with the least possible movement

◆ remove him from the cold environment, e.g. water, snow, poorly heated housing to a warm shelter

◆ **remove** wet clothing and place the casualty under warm covers, such as a warm sleeping bag

◆ **protect him from the wind** by huddling with the casualty

◆ give the conscious casualty a **warm sweet drink**. Do not give alcohol or coffee or other caffeine-containing drinks

◆ **monitor** breathing and pulse

◆ if breathing is ineffective, provide assisted breathing

Huddling

Warm sweet drink

12

A man is pulled from an icy lake and placed in a shelter. He is conscious and shivering. Place the following first aid actions in the **appropriate sequence of performance.** Write the numbers in the boxes provided.

☐ A. Wrap him in warm blankets.

☐ B. Watch his breathing and check his pulse often.

☐ C. Give him a hot drink with sugar.

☐ D. Take off his wet clothes carefully.

A.2 B.4 C.3 D.1

13

When the casualty becomes unconscious:

- ◆ obtain medical help immediately
- ◆ carefully cut off wet clothing and cover the casualty. The slightest rough handling may cause his heart to fail
- ◆ give artificial respiration if breathing stops, but handle the casualty gently.
- ◆ ventilate at an appropriate rate for the age of the casualty
- ◆ **check for signs of circulation for 1 to 2 minutes** to ensure that even a weak, slow pulse can be detected
- ◆ do not attempt **active rewarming**, unless medical help is delayed

If signs of circulation are not present:

- ◆ **give CPR only if it can be maintained** without interruption until medical help takes over
- ◆ if no medical help is available, continue to ventilate until the casualty is re-warmed

Never assume that a casualty in severe hypothermia is dead until his body is warm again and there are still no signs of life.

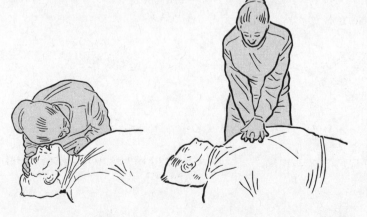

Check for pulse   CPR

First aid for cold injuries—review

14

1. Your friend has severe frostbite on both feet. You are in a remote area in a warm lodge, but **without access to medical help**. Which of the following first aid actions should you do? Check ☑ your answer.

☐ A. Help the casualty walk until his feet are rewarmed.

☐ B. Gently rewarm the frozen feet in warm water of about 40°C (104°F).

☐ C. Ask the casualty to rub his feet vigorously.

☐ D. Give the casualty a glass of hot rum to drink.

2. Which of the following actions would be correct first aid for a **non-breathing** casualty suffering from severe hypothermia? Check ☑ your answers.

☐ A. Take 1 to 2 minutes to check for a pulse (there is a very faint pulse).

☐ B. Handle the casualty gently and give CPR.

☐ C. Get medical help immediately.

☐ D. Handle the casualty gently and give AR.

1.B 2.A 2.C 2.D

Heat illnesses

15

Heat cramps, heat exhaustion and heatstroke are illnesses that are caused by:

- the body's inability to maintain a normal temperature of 37°C (98.6°F)
- long exposure to hot conditions
- overexposure to the sun
- lack of fluids to replace lost body fluids
- vigorous exercise or hard labour in a hot environment

To **prevent heat illnesses,** you should:

- expose the body gradually to a hot environment
- protect the head from direct sunshine
- drink sufficient water to replace body fluids lost through sweating
- avoid long periods of work or exercise in a hot environment

Drinking fluids

16

Which of the following precautions would help you to avoid illness from exposure to heat?

Check ☑ the correct answers.

☐ A. Take drinks when you are working in the heat.

☐ B. Avoid wearing a hat on a hot sunny day to allow body heat to be lost through the head.

☐ C. If you are not used to a hot climate or workplace, stay in the heat for only a short time.

☐ D. Take frequent breaks in a cool place when you are working or playing on a hot day.

Heat cramps

17

Heat cramps are painful muscle spasms caused by an excessive loss of salt and water during sweating. This condition is not serious and usually responds well to first aid.

You may see:

◆ excessive sweating

The casualty may complain of:

◆ painful muscle cramps in the legs and abdomen

Stomach cramps

First aid for heat cramps

When a person is complaining of heat cramps, you should:

◆ place her in a **cool place** to rest
◆ give her **water** to drink, as much as she will take
◆ obtain medical help if muscle pain continues

Place in shade

Giving
water to drink

Heat exhaustion

. . . .

18

Heat exhaustion is more serious than heat cramps.

It occurs when excessive sweating causes a loss of body fluids and when a hot environment and high humidity do not allow the body to cool by sweating.

Excessive sweating

You may see signs of shock:

◆ excessive sweating
◆ cold, clammy, pale skin
◆ weak and rapid pulse
◆ rapid, shallow breathing
◆ vomiting
◆ unconsciousness

The casualty may complain of:

◆ blurred vision
◆ dizziness
◆ headache
◆ nausea
◆ painful cramps in the legs and abdomen

Painful cramps

Suspect heat exhaustion when the casualty is found in high heat and humidity and shows signs of shock with no indications of injury or illness.

. . . .

19

When a casualty is suffering from heat exhaustion, which of the following signs and symptoms may be present?

Check ☑ your answers in the boxes provided.

☐ A. The skin is whitish, cool and damp.
☐ B. The pulse and breathing are very slow.
☐ C. She tells you that she has a sore head and feels sick to her stomach.
☐ D. She has difficulty walking because her legs hurt.
☐ E. She collapses and does not respond.

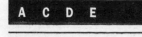

20

First aid for heat exhaustion

The first aid for heat exhaustion is a combination of the first aid for heat cramps and shock.

If the casualty is fully conscious, you should:

- place the casualty at rest in a cool place, with feet and legs elevated
- remove excessive clothing
- loosen tight clothing at neck and waist
- give water to drink, as much as the casualty will take
- if the casualty is vomiting, give nothing by mouth, ensure an open airway and get medical help immediately

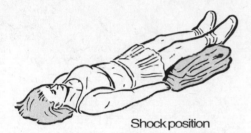

Shock position

Give water to drink

If the casualty is unconscious:

- obtain medical help immediately
- place the casualty into the recovery position
- monitor ABC's and give life-saving first aid as needed
- give ongoing casualty care until medical help takes over

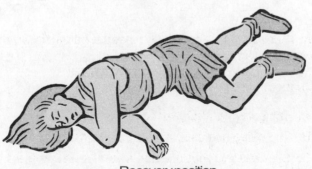

Recovery position

Heatstroke

. . . .

21

Heatstroke is life-threatening. There are two kinds of heatstroke:

◆ **classic** heatstroke occurs when the body's temperature control fails

◆ **exertional** heatstroke occurs as a result of heavy physical exertion in high temperature

You may see:

◆ body temperature rising rapidly to 40°C (104°F) and above

◆ rapid and full pulse, becoming weaker in later stages

◆ flushed, hot, **dry skin in classic** heatstroke

◆ flushed, hot, **sweaty skin in exertional** heatstroke

◆ noisy breathing

◆ vomiting

◆ restlessness

◆ convulsions

◆ unconsciousness

The casualty may complain of:

◆ headache

◆ dizziness

◆ nausea

Dizziness

Flushed, hot,
dry skin

Flushed, hot,
sweaty skin

Elderly persons and those in poor health are more likely to suffer from heatstroke.

22

First aid for heatstroke

Heatstroke is a high priority emergency. **It is life-threatening.**

◆ Send for medical help immediately

To prevent permanent brain damage or death, you must **reduce the body temperature quickly.**

You should:

◆ move the person to a cool, shaded place

◆ ensure a clear airway and adequate breathing

◆ remove clothing

◆ **immerse** the casualty **in a cool bath** and watch her closely, or

◆ **sponge** the casualty **with cool water, or place cold packs or** cold compresses in the armpit, neck and groin areas, or

◆ **cover her with wet sheets** and fan cool air over her

◆ when the body feels cooler to the touch, cover her with a dry sheet

◆ monitor the casualty's temperature and if it rises, repeat the cooling procedure

◆ give ongoing casualty care until hand over to medical help

◆ place the unconscious casualty into the **recovery position**

◆ place the conscious casualty into the **shock position**

Immerse in cool bath

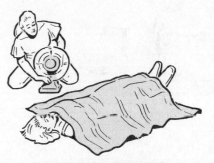

Sponge with cool water

Shock position and air fan

23

A casualty is suffering from heatstroke. You have sent for medical help. While awaiting medical help, which of the following actions could you take to reduce her body temperature?

Check ☑ your answers in the boxes provided.

☐ A. Place cold, wet cloths on her forehead, the back of her neck, under the armpits and around her groin.

☐ B. Apply a cold dry towel to her forehead.

☐ C. Place cool, wet bath sheets over her body and circulate air around her.

☐ D. Soak her in a large tub filled with ice water.

☐ E. Place her feet in a pail of tepid water.

When the temperature has been reduced:

☐ F. Position her to ensure an open airway and watch her carefully.

☐ G. Leave her to herself to get a good rest.

Recovery position

A C F

Notes

. . . .

EMERGENCY CHILDBIRTH AND MISCARRIAGE

Introduction to emergency childbirth

1

A basic knowledge of the female reproductive system and its relationship to the unborn child will help to give assistance during an emergency delivery.

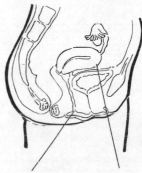

Vagina   Uterus

- ◆ **Fetus** — the developing baby

- ◆ **Uterus** — the hollow muscular structure, also called womb, inside which the fetus develops

- ◆ **Cervix** — the neck of the uterus through which the fetus will pass into the vagina

- ◆ **Amniotic sac** — a fluid-filled sac, contained within the uterus, in which the fetus develops

- ◆ **Amniotic fluid** — liquid that surrounds and protects the fetus in the amniotic sac

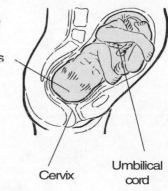

Fetus

Cervix   Umbilical cord

- ◆ **Placenta** — large flat, spongy organ that is attached to the wall of the uterus and supplies the fetus with nutrients and oxygen from the mother

- ◆ **Umbilical cord** — a rope-like structure that contains blood vessels and connects the placenta with the fetus

- ◆ **Vagina** — the muscular birth canal for the delivery of the infant

Labour

. . . .

2

Labour is the process through which the body prepares itself to deliver the baby.

The **early signs of labour beginning** are signalled by:

◆ regular rhythmic contractions at first mild to moderate strength

◆ breaking of the amniotic sac and the release of fluid through the vagina, known as "the water breaking"

◆ appearance of the "bloody show", consisting of blood and mucus, from the vagina

Normally the beginning of labour gives enough warning for the mother to be transported to a medical facility for delivery.

There are **three stages** of labour:

1. **opening of the cervix** (widening) brought about by increasingly stronger contractions
2. **birth of the baby**
3. **delivery of the placenta**

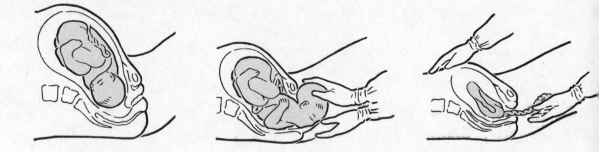

. . . .

3

Which of the following are normal signs indicating that a pregnant woman is beginning labour?

Check ☑ the correct answers.

☐ A. A gush or trickle of watery fluid from the vagina.

☐ B. Frequent urination.

☐ C. A steady flow of blood from the vagina.

☐ D. Sharp pains felt in the abdomen.

☐ E. A pinkish discharge from the vagina.

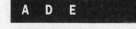

Signs of imminent delivery

4

Signs and symptoms of imminent delivery are:

◆ long, strong contractions, less than 2 minutes apart

◆ the mother's previous experience. If she says, the baby is coming, believe her!

◆ bulging of the vaginal opening and seeing the baby's head (crowning)

◆ the mother is straining and pushing down, feels as though she has to have a bowel movement

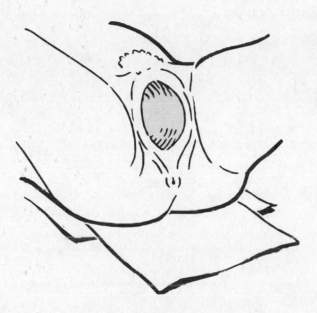

Crowning

5

Mark each statement below as true **(T)** or false **(F)**.

☐ A. The urge of the mother to move her bowels is an indication that the baby is about to be born.

☐ B. Intense pain in short intervals usually means that the baby will be delivered very soon.

☐ C. When the baby's head can be seen through the vagina, there is still time to transport the mother to the hospital.

☐ D. A woman who has given birth before can usually tell when the delivery is about to occur.

A.T B.T C.F D.T

Preparation for emergency delivery

6

To prepare for an emergency delivery:

◆   try to get medical help, or

◆   locate an assistant, preferably the father or a woman

◆   assemble the necessary materials, e.g.:
  ❖   clean towels, sheets
  ❖   baby blanket
  ❖   sterile tape or narrow roller bandage to tie off the cord
  ❖   absorbent material to absorb vaginal bleeding after delivery

◆   container for placenta

◆   soap, water and towels to wash your hands

◆   gloves, sterile, if possible

Some of these items such as diapers, receiving blanket, may be found in the materials that the mother has packed for the hospital.

7

To **prepare the mother** for delivery:

◆   provide reassurance, comfort and **privacy**

◆   during labour, let the mother find the position of most comfort, usually on the left side. (If she wants to lie on her back, place a folded towel under her right hip. This will help shift the baby off the mother's main blood vessels.)

◆   when birth is imminent, place the mother on her back with knees bent and head supported on a pillow, unless she prefers another position

◆   place clean sheets or towels under her buttocks and between her thighs

◆   cover her with sheets or towels so that you can easily lift the cover to check the progress of labour

First aid during delivery

8

In preparing for the emergency delivery, keep in mind that **the aims** are to:

◆ **assist** the mother in delivering her baby

◆ **protect** the **mother and baby** during and after delivery until they are handed over to medical help

◆ **send** all parts of the placenta and layers of the amniotic sac to the hospital with the mother

Do not interfere with the natural birth process, particularly during the last stage of labour.

The baby's head will usually be born first. If the head comes out too quickly, the baby may be harmed and the mother injured.

To prevent injury to the baby:

◆ tell the mother **to control** her **pushing**. Ask her to try panting—that helps to prevent the urge to bear down

◆ use **very gentle control** with the palm of your hand on the baby's head to slow its delivery

◆ once the head is delivered, ask the mother to **stop pushing**

◆ check the neck area for the umbilical cord; if not present ask the mother to continue pushing

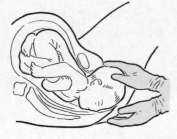  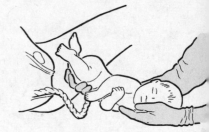

As the baby is being delivered, carefully support the head and body. Remember, the baby is wet and slippery.

9

Check ☑ the correct statements regarding first aid during the birth of a baby.

☐ A. Delivery is a natural process accomplished by the mother's body.

☐ B. Your role, as a first aider, is to ensure the safety of the mother and the infant.

☐ C. Once the top of the head is visible, tell the mother to press down harder.

☐ D. Place both hands around the baby's head and pull it out of the birth canal.

☐ E. Gently and securely hold the newborn when it is emerging from the birth canal.

10

A baby may be born with the **umbilical cord** around his neck.

◆   **Check** the infant's neck

Should the umbilical cord be wrapped around the neck:

◆   ask the mother **to stop pushing**
◆   **slide** your fingers under the cord and loosen it gently

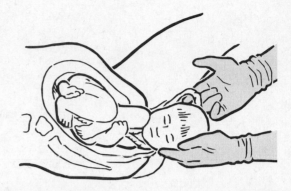

There should be enough slack to allow you to:

◆   **slip** the cord over the baby's head or the upper shoulder

Do not pull or exert force on the cord.

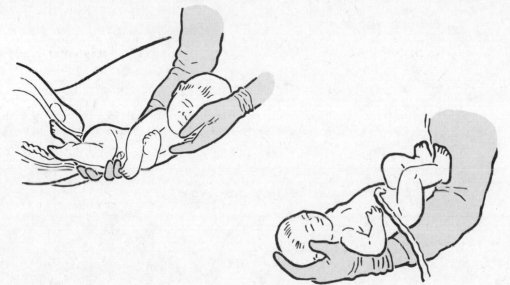

11

Which of the following procedures should you do if a baby is born with the umbilical cord around his neck?

Check ☑ the correct answers.

☐   A.   Cut the cord immediately.
☐   B.   Loosen the cord gently.
☐   C.   Pull the baby's head through the loop of the cord.
☐   D.   Ease the cord away from the baby's neck.
☐   E.   Support the baby's head during the procedure.
☐   F.   Wait for medical help to remove the cord.

Care of the new-born baby

. . . .

12

Newborns are covered with a whitish, **slippery coating** that makes them difficult to hold. Handle the baby **firmly**, **carefully** and **gently** and keep her at **birth canal level** until the umbilical cord stops pulsating.

- ◆ Note and record the time of birth
- ◆ Keep the baby on her side with the head lower than the body to clear fluids from the airway
- ◆ Wipe the baby's face to clear mucus from the nose and mouth

The baby will probably breathe and cry almost immediately.

- ◆ If the baby does not breathe on her own, stimulate the baby by rubbing the back gently or by slapping the soles of the feet . **Do not** hang the baby upside down by her heels and slap her on the back or buttocks
- ◆ Start mouth-to-mouth-and-nose AR if there is no response
- ◆ Start CPR if there are no signs of circulation

 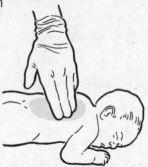

When the baby is breathing and crying, and the cord stops pulsating:

- ◆ dry the baby with a towel, but do **not remove** the slippery coating; it will be absorbed
- ◆ keep the baby warm
- ◆ place the baby on her side on the mother's abdomen, with head lowered
- ◆ continue to watch baby's breathing and wait for the placenta to be delivered

Care of the umbilical cord and placenta

13

The **umbilical cord** connects the baby to the placenta. The **placenta** will usually be delivered within 20 minutes following the baby's birth.

- **Never attempt to force delivery of the placenta by pulling on the cord**

To assist:

- gently massage the mother's lower abdomen to stimulate contractions
- catch the placenta in a clean towel, bag or basin
- ensure that all parts of the placenta are saved
- keep the placenta at the same level as the newborn
- place the placenta in a clean towel and wrap it with the infant for transportation to the hospital

If medical help is close by and there is no obvious bleeding from the placenta, do not tie or cut the umbilical cord!

If there is **obvious bleeding** from the placenta, **act quickly!**

- **Place 2 ties** 7.5 cm (3 inches) apart, 15 to 30 cm (6 to 12 inches) from the baby's navel, using a clean tape or heavy string. **Take care not to cut the cord with the tie!**
- Keep the placenta at the same level as the newborn
- Transport as soon as possible to the hospital

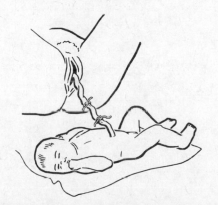

Care of the mother after delivery

14

To care for the mother after delivery of the placenta:

◆ examine the skin between the anus and vagina for tears (injury) and apply pressure to the wounds

◆ remove soiled sheet

◆ place sanitary pads over the vagina to absorb bleeding

◆ massage the lower abdomen every 5–10 minutes to help the uterus contract and control bleeding

◆ let the baby suck from her mother's breasts; this will help to keep the uterus contracted

◆ position the mother comfortably and keep her warm

◆ give emotional support and arrange for transportation as soon as possible

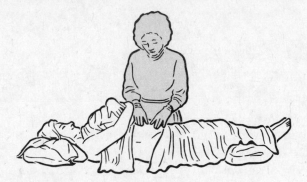

Should the bleeding from the vagina be excessive:

◆ continue massaging the lower abdomen every 5–10 minutes

◆ place the mother into the shock position

◆ keep the mother and the baby warm

◆ transport immediately to the closest medical facility

Do not use
a pillow if
bleeding is
severe

Miscarriage

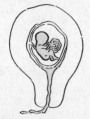

15

Miscarriage, also called **spontaneous abortion,** is the natural loss of the fetus before it is capable of survival outside the uterus (before the twentieth week of pregnancy).

Miscarriage can be classified into 3 types

Threatened miscarriage   Inevitable miscarriage   Complete miscarriage

Signs and symptoms

The woman, knowing or suspecting that she is pregnant, may complain of:

- vaginal bleeding, often heavy
- cramp-like pains in the lower abdomen
- backache
- passage of tissue

Emergency Care

- Give first aid for shock
- Place casualty into the shock position or on her left side
- Transport to the nearest medical facility as soon as possible
- Take any passed tissue or evidence of blood loss (bloody sheets, towels, underwear) to the hospital for the examining doctor
- Provide emotional support

Do not use a pillow if bleeding is severe

Keep the woman warm

Notes

● ●

AUTOMATED EXTERNAL DEFIBRILLATION-AED

Automated external defibrillation, the application of an electric shock to a heart that has stopped beating, has been proven to be one of the most important tools in saving the lives of sudden cardiac arrest casualties. New technology has resulted in machines that are truly portable, safe, easy to use and easy to maintain. As these devices become more popular and as more students are trained in their use, the survival rate for cardiac arrest will increase dramatically.

Cardiac Conduction System

1

The heart has very specialized cells that generate electrical impulses. These impulses are what cause the heart to have a rhythmic pumping action. They cause the atria and ventricles to contract and relax thereby allowing blood into the heart and forcing it out to circulate throughout the body.

sinoatrial node (pacemaker)

atrioventricular node

The impulse begins in an area in the atria called the sinoatrial node. This area of the heart is also known as the pacemaker for it is the master electrical controller. From here the impulse travels through the atria to another node called the atrioventricular node where it then travels through the ventricles. This wave of electricity as it passes through the heart can be measured and this is what is seen on an electrocardiogram or ECG.

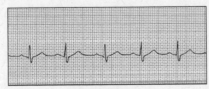

Normal ECG

When a person has a heart attack or other cardiac event , depending on how much of the heart muscle is damaged, these electrical impulses can be disturbed and the rhythm can become very chaotic. Four different types of abnormal rhythms are important to understand when learning about AEDs.

Ventricular Fibrillation (VF). VF is the most common rhythm seen in cardiac arrest casualties. Instead of beating in a strong regular fashion, the heart quivers much like a bowl of jelly. As a result the heart is not able to pump blood to the body and the casualty will not have a pulse. Ventricular fibrillation, if not corrected, will result in death.

Ventricular fibrillation and ventricular tachycardia can both be corrected by using an AED.

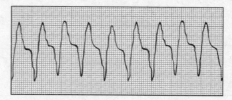

ECG-Ventricular Fibrillation

Pulseless Ventricular Tachycardia (VT). This is a very fast heart rate (above 180 beats per minute) that also interferes with the pumping action of the heart. VT without a pulse is a life- threatening rhythm and like VF must be corrected as soon as possible.

ECG—Ventricular Tachycardia

Asystole. Asystole is a condition in which where there is no electrical activity in the heart at all- the so-called flat line on an ECG.

Pulseless Electrical Activity (PEA). In PEA you would see what looks like a normal heart rhythm on the ECG but in fact there would be no pulse. This often occurs in trauma casualties where so much blood is lost that the heart is pumping but there is no fluid left to pump.

It is important to know about these last two rhythms because AEDs will not shock asystole or PEA.

2

Of the following sentences, check ☑ each true statement.

☐ A. The heart has specialized cells that generate electricity

☐ B. Ventricular fibrillation can cause death if not corrected

☐ C. Heart attacks always cause ventricular fibrillation

☐ D. Ventricular tachycardia is a very fast heart rate

How Do AEDs Work?

3

AEDs are computerized defibrillators. They are programmed to recognize and shock two types of heart rhythms, VF and pulseless VT. If the machine recognizes either VT or VF in a casualty it will charge and will indicate, usually by a voice prompt, that a shock is advised.

You cannot accidently shock a heart that is in normal rhythm

When the shock is delivered to the heart a number of things happen. First the shock will momentarily stop all electrical activity in the heart. This means that the VT or VF that is occurring will be quickly terminated. When this occurs, it gives the heart's pacemaker, the sinoatrial node, a chance to take command again and begin generating the impulses which will start the heart's normal pumping action.

This may not occur with the first shock and indeed in some cases many shocks are necessary to help the heart regain its normal function. It is important to remember that AEDs will only shock when VT or VF is present. You **cannot** accidently shock a heart that is in normal rhythm, nor will the machine shock asystole or PEA.

Time — The Crucial Factor

4

Time is a critical factor in determining survival from cardiac arrest. As you know from the Chain of Survival, CPR should be started within four minutes to help prevent brain damage. Defibrillation must also be perfomed early, ideally within eight minutes to be most effective. The reason for this is that the heart will only stay in fibrillation a short time before all electrical activity ceases. Once this occurs, the heart is in asystole and as noted above, AEDs will not shock asystole. Also, the longer the heart is in fibrillation, the greater the amount of heart muscle that will die because of the lack of oxygen to the heart tissue. Therefore quick defibrillation means more heart muscle saved in cardiac arrest casualties. Studies have shown that for each minute that defibrillation is delayed, the chance of survival declines by up to ten percent.

Time = Muscle

Few cardiac arrest casualties survive if defibrillation is delayed longer than twelve minutes.

The Role of CPR in AED

5

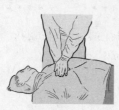

CPR Buys Time

In most cases CPR alone will not restart the heart . It is however an important part of the Chain of Survival. Not only does it keep oxygenated blood flowing to the brain, it also helps extend the length of time that the heart will remain in VT or VF. This is important because these are the only types of rhythms that AEDs will shock. CPR then can "buy some time" for the casualty until the AED is attached and ready to deliver a shock.

How to Use an AED

6

1. Press the POWER ON button.
   - ◆ Connect cables to AED.
   - ◆ Attach cables to electrode pads (with some models both are pre-connected.)
2. Attach adhesive electrode pads to the casualty's chest.
   - ◆ Bare the chest.
   - ◆ Shave the chest if necessary where the pads will be placed. Otherwise you may have trouble getting the pads to adhere properly if the casualty has a very hairy chest.
   - ◆ Dry the chest if necessary. Pads adhere better to a dry surface.
   - ◆ Peel away the protective plastic and attach electrode pads — one pad on the right upper anterior side of the casualty's chest just below the collarbone and one pad on the left lower anterior chest wall just below the nipple. Some electrodes have instructions on where they should be placed.

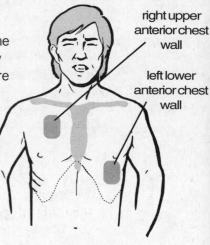

right upper anterior chest wall

left lower anterior chest wall

defibrillator pad sites

3. Stand back and ensure no one is touching the casualty (clear casualty).
4. Press the ANALYZE button on the defibrillator and follow the voice prompts (note-some machines automatically analyze when the power is turned on).

Once the machine has analyzed the heart rhythm it will indicate either shock required or no shock required. On the following page you will see the shock—no shock protocols.

Protocol sequences for shockable and non-shockable rhythms.

7   Assess responsivness. If unresponsive call or send for medical help and get AED. After establishing no signs of circulation and connecting AED to casualty, one of the following protocols will apply.

Shockable Rhythm

Clear casualty; ANALYZE
Shock Indicated
Clear casualty; SHOCK

Clear casualty; ANALYZE
Shock Indicated
Clear casualty; SHOCK

Clear casualty; ANALYZE
Shock Indicated
Clear casualty; SHOCK

Check signs of circulation
If no signs of circulation
CPR for 1 minute

Repeat set of three shocks
(if indicated)

Check signs of circulation
If no signs of circulation
CPR for 1 minute

Repeat set of three shocks
(if indicated)

Continue sequence of 3 shocks
and CPR until medical help takes
over

Note: If AED advises " No Shock",
go to Non-Shockable Rhythm
protocol

Non-Shockable Rhythm

Clear casualty; ANALYZE
No shock indicated

Check signs of circulation
If no signs of circulation
CPR for 1 minute

Clear casualty; ANALYZE
No shock indicated

Check signs of circulation
If no signs of circulation
CPR for 1 minute

Clear casualty; ANALYZE

Check signs of circulation
If no signs of circulation
CPR for 1 minute

Continue CPR until medical help
takes over

Note: If AED advises "Shock", go to
Shockable Rhythm protocol

Post-Resuscitation Care & Handover to EMS

8

If defibrillation is successful and the casualty regains a pulse you may be faced with two situations. First, the casualty may start breathing on his or her own but remain unresponsive. In this case place the casualty into the recovery position and monitor the ABCs. Second, the casualty may have a pulse but may not be breathing. In this case start artificial respiration. In either situation leave the AED attached-some machines continually monitor heart rhythms or you may need to use the device if the casualty's heart stops again.

Certain information is important for ambulance or fire personnel such as the time of collapse, time when CPR was started, time when first shock was delivered and number of shocks. Provide as much detail as possible and follow the directions of medical personnel once they arrive on the scene.

Defibrillation—Special Considerations and Special Circumstances

9

As mentioned previously, AEDs will only shock VF and VT. There are several other important considerations to be aware of when using these devices.

AEDS and Children. AEDs are not meant to be used in young children. As a guideline their use should be restricted to casualties over the age of eight who weigh more than 25 kilograms (55 lbs.). This may vary in different areas—follow local protocols.

AEDs in Pregnant Patients. AEDs can be used in all stages of pregnancy.

AEDs in Trauma Casualties. AEDs are not recommended for cardiac arrest caused by trauma. If however, you suspect that the trauma was the result of a cardiac event, for example an elderly gentleman riding a bicycle has a heart attack, falls off the bicycle and injures himself, you may choose to use an AED. Use your best judgment in cases such as these.

AEDS and Pacemakers or Implanted Defibrillators. Some people have pacemakers implanted under their skin to help the heart maintain a normal rhythm. Defibrillator pads should not be placed directly over the pacemaker site but should be approximately one inch away. Similarly, other people have a small defibrillator implanted under their skin which will automatically deliver a shock to the heart if VF or VT is detected. Again you should not place your defibrillator pads over the implanted device. If you see minor contractions in the chest area while you are getting ready to defibrillate, wait 20-30 seconds until the patient's implanted defibrillator is finished. You can touch the casualty while his implanted defibrillator is shocking without danger to yourself.

implanted pacemaker sites

implanted defibrillator site

AEDS and Hypothermic Casualties. In the severely hypothermic casualty, limit the number of shocks to a maximum of three.

AEDS and Patch Medications. Some casualties wear a patch that contains medication such as nitroglycerin for angina. If you see a patch gently remove it from the chest and wipe the area clean. Handle the patch carefully to avoid being affected yourself by the medication.

AEDS in a Wet Environment. Because AEDs generate electricity, you need to be careful in wet environments. Move the casualty to a dry area if possible and wipe the chest with a towel or cloth. If you or the casualty is submersed in water, avoiding using an AED.

AEDS on Metal Surfaces. It is best if casualties are on non-conductive surfaces but you should not be at risk if you have to use a device on a casualty who is on a metal surface.

AEDS in Moving Vehicles. If you are transporting a casualty who is connected to an AED, stop the vehicle if you need to use the device. Sometimes, the motion of the vehicle can trick the AED into thinking that VT or VF is present and it may advise a shock when it is not needed.

Stop vehicle before using an AED

AED Troubleshooting and Maintenance. Sometimes the device will indicate "Check Electrodes". If this occurs, check the cable to pads connection, the cable to machine connection and the adherence of the pads to the casualty's chest particularly if the casualty has a very hairy chest or If the chest was wet prior to attaching the pads.

Machines will also advise if motion is detected or if the battery is low. AEDs are sold with an instruction manual that will outline troubleshooting in detail.

While AEDs are becoming easier to use and maintain, regular maintenance and operational checks are required and will help avoid problems when you have to use the device on a casualty. Follow the manufacturer's suggested schedule and checklist.

* * *

LO

Mark each statement below as true (**T**) or false (**F**):

- ☐ A. When an AED delivers a shock, all electrical activity in the heart momentarily ceases.
- ☐ B. The heart will remain in ventricular fibrillation for an indefinite amount of time.
- ☐ C. In hypothermic casualties , limit the number of shocks to a maximum of five.
- ☐ D. If you have to transport a casualty who is connected to an AED, stop the vehicle before using the device.
- ☐ E. AEDS will shock VF, VT and PEA.

A.T B.F C.F D.T E.F

Notes

Legal Aspects of Providing AED

. . . .

11

Completion of a course in automated external defibrillation does not automatically certify you to perform this procedure on a cardiac arrest casualty. Currently In many areas of Canada, defibrillation is considered to be a medical act. This means that permission to use these devices must be given by a physician. The doctor, in effect, delegates the responsibility to persons in whom he or she is confident will operate the machine safely and appropriately on a casualty. Please read the following Statement of Understanding, sign it and have your Instructor sign it. If you have any questions on the use of AEDs in your province, ask your Instructor for clarification.

Statement of Understanding

The performance of automated external defibrillation on a sudden cardiac arrest casualty is a controlled medical act that must by delegated to you by a physician. You will be permitted to operate an AED under the license and written direction of this physician. Because AED providers operate under the medical license of the delegating physician, he or she has the final authority over local defibrillation protocols, retraining requirements, and use of AED documentation and reporting.

Wherever possible St. John Ambulance will ensure that the information that you receive on this program will be compatible with what you will be expected to do when you seek authorization from a physician as a defibrillation provider.

I understand that completion of this St. John Ambulance automated external defibrillation program qualifies me to perform this procedure on casualties only with written authorization from a physician to use this device in cardiac arrest situations.

Name (please print) _____

Date _____

Your Signature _____

Instructor's Signature _____

Emergency scene management—Unresponsive casualty

An unconscious adult casualty is lying face up. The first aider witnessed the casualty's collapse.
There is a bystander nearby.

Activity

Performance Guidelines

SCENE SURVEY

- take charge of the situation

- call out for help and assess hazards at the scene

- determine the number of casualties, what happened, and the mechanism of injury

- identify yourself and offer to help

- assess responsiveness

- send for medical help

Approach from within the casualty's line of sight

Ask bystanders to standby. Make the area safe. To protect yourself, put on latex or vinyl gloves if available

Since you witnessed the incident, you know what happened and the mechanism of injury [You do not suspect head or spinal injuries]

Identify yourself and ask for consent. If the casualty doesn't respond, you have implied consent

Ask, "Are you O.K.?" and gently tap the casualty's shoulders
[Casualty does not respond]

Give the following information: what happened, location, and that the casualty is unresponsive

PRIMARY SURVEY (ABCs)

- airway

- breathing

- circulation

A Open the airway using the head-tilt, chin-lift

B Look, listen and feel for up to 10 seconds to check for breathing
[Casualty is breathing]

Assess the quality and the rate of breathing by placing a hand on the casualty's chest
[Breathing is quiet, occurs without effort and with an even, steady rhythm]

C Check skin condition and temperature
[Skin is pale, warm and dry]

Check for hidden, severe, external bleeding and signs of internal bleeding using the rapid body survey [Casualty has no apparent bleeding or deformities]

SECONDARY SURVEY

ONGOING CASUALTY CARE

- monitor casualty's condition

- record the events

- report on what happened

[Secondary survey is not required as medical help will arrive soon]

Reassure the casualty and loosen tight clothing at the neck, chest and waist.
Place the casualty into the **recovery position.**
If possible, place a blanket underneath the casualty before turning.
Cover the casualty, do not give anything by mouth. Protect the casualty's belongings

Reassess ABCs

Take notes of the casualty's condition and any changes that may occur

Tell medical attendants what happened. [Casualty remains unconscious]

Emergency scene management—Responsive casualty

An adult casualty has fallen and hit her head, and is lying face up. The casualty can speak clearly and open her eyes when spoken to. Two bystanders are present who witnessed the incident.

Activity

Performance Guidelines

SCENE SURVEY

- take charge of the situation

Approach from within the casualty's line of sight. Tell the casualty not to move

- call out for help

Ask bystanders to standby

- assess hazards at the scene

Make the area safe. To protect yourself, put on latex or vinyl gloves if available

- determine the number of casualties, what happened, and the mechanism of injury

Question the casualty to determine what happened and the mechanism of injury *[Head/spinal injuries are suspected]*

- identify yourself and offer to help

Identify yourself and ask for consent

- send for medical help

Give the following information: what happened, location, and the condition of the casualty

- assess responsiveness

Provide support for the casualty's head and neck since head/spinal injuries are suspected—ask, "Are you OK?" *[A conscious casualty **is** responsive]*

PRIMARY SURVEY (ABCs)

- airway

A   Ask the casualty, "Where are you hurt?" *[The casualty can speak clearly therefore has a clear airway]*

Instruct a bystander to steady and support the casualty's head and neck

- breathing

B   Check for effectiveness of breathing. Ask, "How is your breathing?" *[The casualty moans.]* Place a hand on the casualty's chest and count the number of breaths per minute *[Breathing is effective]*

- circulation

C   Check skin condition and temperature *[skin is pale, warm and dry]* Check for hidden, severe, external bleeding and signs of internal bleeding with the rapid body survey *[Casualty has no apparent bleeding or deformities]*

SECONDARY SURVEY

[Secondary survey is not required as medical help will arrive soon]

ONGOING CASUALTY CARE

Continue support for the head and neck and do not move the casualty

Reassure the casualty and loosen tight clothing at the neck, chest and waist. Cover the casualty. Do not give anything by mouth

- monitor casualty's condition

Recheck ABCs often

- record the events

Take notes of the casualty's condition and any changes that may occur—protect the casualty's belongings

- report on what happened

Tell medical attendants what happened, the casualty's condition and what first aid was given *[Casualty remains conscious]*

Recovery position—Walk around method

An unconscious adult casualty is lying face up with no apparent injuries. There is a bystander. The scene survey and primary survey have been performed.

Activity	Performance Guidelines
SCENE SURVEY	
• take charge of the situation	You have taken charge
• call out for help	You have called out for help and a bystander responded
• assess hazards at the scene	You have made the area safe
• determine the number of casualties, what happened, and the mechanism of injury	You have questioned the bystander *(You do not suspect head/spinal injuries)*
• identify yourself and offer to help	You have identified yourself and asked for consent
• assess responsiveness	You have assessed responsiveness *[The casualty is unresponsive]*
• send for medical help	A bystander has been sent to call medical help
PRIMARY SURVEY (ABCs)	
• airway	A [The casualty has an open airway]
• breathing	B [The casualty is breathing effectively]
• circulation	C [The casualty is not bleeding but is in shock]
SECONDARY SURVEY	*[Secondary survey is not required as medical help will arrive soon]*
ONGOING CASUALTY CARE	
• give first aid for shock	**Reassure**. Loosen tight clothing. Place into the **recovery position**. **Cover**. Do not give anything by mouth
• monitor casualty's condition	Check ABCs often
• record the events	Take notes. Protect belongings
• report on what happened	Tell medical attendants the casualty's condition and the first aid given *(Casualty remains unconscious)*

Artificial respiration—Adult

An adult casualty is lying face down. The first aider witnessed the incident. A bystander is present.

Activity

SCENE SURVEY

- take charge of the situation
- call out for help and assess hazards

- determine the number of casualties, what happened, and the mechanism of injury
- identify yourself and offer to help
- assess responsiveness

- send for medical help

PRIMARY SURVEY (ABCs)

- airway
- breathing

- circulation

- Complete the primary survey
  check effectiveness of breathing
  check circulation

SECONDARY SURVEY
ONGOING CASUALTY CARE

- give first aid for shock

- monitor casualty's condition and record the events

- report on what happened

Performance Guidelines

Approach from within the casualty's line of sight

Ask the bystander to standby. Make the area safe. To protect yourself, put on latex or vinyl gloves if available

Since you witnessed the incident, you know what happened and the mechanism of injury *[You do not suspect head or spinal injuries]*

Identify yourself and ask for consent. If the casualty doesn't respond, you have implied consent

Ask, "Are you O.K.?" and gently tap the casualty's shoulders *[Casualty does not respond]*

Give the following information: what happened, location, and that the casualty is unresponsive

Turn the casualty onto her back

A Open the airway using the head-tilt chin-lift

B Look, listen and feel for up to 10 seconds to check for breathing
[Casualty is not breathing]
Give two slow breaths (2 seconds each) using enough air to make the chest rise
Use a pocket mask or face shield, if available
[The chest rises and falls]

C Check for signs of circulation (pulse, movement, coughing, etc.) for no more than 10 seconds
[There are signs of circulation]

Continue ventilations. One slow breath every five seconds for about one minute

Maintain head tilt and recheck for signs of circulation for up to 10 seconds after one minute (and every few minutes thereafter)
(The casualty is now breathing]

Check the rate, rhythm and quality of breathing
[Breathing is effective)

Check for shock. A rapid body survey is not required as other injuries are not suspected *[Casualty is in shock]*

[Secondary survey is not required as medical help will arrive soon]

Reassurethe casualty and loosen tight clothing at the neck, chest and waist. Place the casualty into the **recovery position. Cover** the casualty, do not give anything by mouth. Protect belongings

Reassess ABCs. Take notes of the casualty's condition and any changes that may occur

Present an oral report to medical attendants

Artificial respiration using jaw-thrust without head-tilt

A casualty has fallen down stairs and is lying face up, at the bottom of a staircase. A bystander is present.

Activity

SCENE SURVEY

- take charge of the situation

- call out for help and assess hazards at the scene

- determine the number of casualties, what happened, and the mechanism of injury

- identify yourself and offer to help
- send for medical help

- assess responsiveness

PRIMARY SURVEY (ABCs)

- airway
- breathing

- circulation

SECONDARY SURVEY

ONGOING CASUALTY CARE

- give first aid for shock

- monitor casualty's condition and record the events

- report on what happened

Performance Guidelines

Approach from within the casualty's line of sight. Tell the casualty not to move

Ask the bystander to stand by. Make the area safe Tor protect yourself, put on latex or vinyl gloves if available

Question the bystander to determine what happened and the mechanism of injury *[Head/spinal injuries are suspected]*

Identify yourself and ask for consent. If the casualty doesn't respond, you have implied consent

Provide support for the casualty's head and neck since head/spinal injuries are suspected—ask "Are you OK?"

Give the following information: what happened, location, and that the casualty is unresponsive

You do not want to move the casualty unnecessarily because you suspect head/spinal injuries—check for breathing in the position found for up to 10 seconds **before** opening the airway
[Casualty is not breathing]

Position the casualty with the logroll manoeuvre, it necessary

A   Open the airway with the **jaw-thrust without head-tilt**

B   Recheck breathing for up to 10 seconds
[Casualty is still not breathing]
Use a pocket mask or face shield if available, or cover the casualty's mouth with your mouth and seal the nose with your cheek. Give two slow breaths (2 seconds each) using just enough air to make the chest rise
[Chest rises and falls]

C   Maintain support for the head and neck while checking for signs of circulation for no more than 10 seconds
[There is a pulse]

Continue artificial respiration (one breath every five seconds) until the casualty starts breathing, medical help takes over, another first aider takes over, or you are physically exhausted and unable to continue

Recheck for signs of circulation for up to 10 seconds after one minute and every few minutes after that

[Secondary survey is not required as medical help will arrive soon]

Continue support for the head and neck—in this situation **do not** put the casualty into recovery position nor raise the feet because of suspected head/spinal injuries—cover the casualty—protect the casualty's belongings
Be prepared to protect the casualty's airway with the logroll manoeuvre

Reassess ABCs. Take notes of the casualty's condition and any changes that may occur

Present an oral report to medical attendants [Casualty remains unconscious]

Choking–Adult conscious becoming unconscious

An adult casualty is grasping at her throat and coughing forcefully. A bystander is present.

Activity	**Performance Guidelines**

SCENE SURVEY

- take charge of the situation

Approach from within the casualty's line of sight

- call out for help and assess hazards at the scene

Ask the bystander to stand by. Make the area safe. To protect yourself, put on latex or vinyl gloves if available

- determine the number of casualties, what happened, and the mechanism of injury

Ask "Are you choking?" *[The casualty is coughing forcefully]*

- identify yourself and offer to help

Identify yourself and ask for consent. If the casualty doesn't respond, you have implied consent

PRIMARY SURVEY (ABCs)

- airway

A Do not intervene at this time—encourage coughing
Watch for signs of complete obstruction

[The casualty now cannot cough, breathe or speak]
When coughing stops, ask "Can you cough?" Stand behind the casualty and landmark—give inward and upward abdominal thrusts until the airway is cleared or the casualty becomes unconscious

[The casualty becomes unconscious]
Ease the casualty to the floor on her back

- send for medical help

Give the following information: what happened, location, and that the casualty is choking and unconscious

Look in the mouth *[Nothing is visible]*

Open the airway and check for breathing *[No breathing]*

Try to ventilate *[Chest does not rise]*

Reposition the head, check the seals and try to ventilate again *[Chest still does not rise]*

Landmark - Give 15 chest compressions. Repeat looking in the mouth, attempts to ventilate and chest compressions until the airway is cleared, medical help takes over or you cannot continue any longer *[The object is seen and removed]*

- breathing

B Give 1 slow breath checking that the chest rises and falls *[Chest rises and falls.]* Give a second breath, watching the chest rise and fall

- circulation

  Complete the primary survey

C Check for signs of circulation for no more than 10 seconds *[The casualty is breathing, but remains unconscious]* Assess the quality and rate of breathing by placing a hand on the casualty's chest. Check circulation (skin temperature and condition). *[Breathing is effective, skin is cold and clammy]*

SECONDARY SURVEY

[Secondary survey is not required as medical help will arrive soon]

ONGOING CASUALTY CARE

Give first aid for shock, monitor casualty's condition. Continue to check ABCs until medical help takes over. Record the events along with any changes that may occur and report to medical attendants when they arrive

Choking–Adult (pregnant or obese)

A woman in an advanced stage of pregnancy appears to be choking and she cannot cough, breathe or speak. A bystander is present.

Activity	Performance Guidelines

Activity

Performance Guidelines

SCENE SURVEY

- take charge of the situation

- call out for help and assess hazards at the scene

- determine the number of casualties, what happened, and the mechanism of injury

- identify yourself and offer to help

PRIMARY SURVEY (ABCs)

- airway

- send for medical help

- breathing

- circulation

  Complete the primary survey

SECONDARY SURVEY

ONGOING CASUALTY CARE

Approach from within the casualty's line of sight

Ask the bystander to stand by. Make the area safe. To protect yourself, put on latex or vinyl gloves if available

Ask "Are you choking?" *[The casualty cannot cough, breathe or speak]*

You have identified yourself and asked for consent. If the casualty doesn't respond, you have implied consent

A   Identify the degree of obstruction

Ask "Can you cough?" Stand behind the casualty and landmark—give inward **chest** thrusts until the airway is cleared or the casualty becomes unconscious

[The casualty becomes unconscious]
Ease the casualty to the floor on her back. Place a wedge under her right hip, if readily available

Give the following information: what happened, location, the number of casualties and that the casualty is choking, and unconscious

Look in the mouth *[Nothing is visible]*

Open the airway and check for breathing *[No breathing]*

Try to ventilate *[Chest does not rise]*

Reposition the head, check the seals and try to ventilate again *[Chest still does not rise]*

Landmark - Give 15 chest compressions—repeat looking in the mouth, attempts to ventilate and chest compressions until the airway is cleared, medical help takes over or you cannot continue any longer *[The object is seen and removed]*

B   Give 1 slow breath checking that the chest rises and falls. *[Chest rises and falls]* Give a second breath, watching the chest rise and fall

C   Check for circulation for no more than 10 seconds. *[The casualty is breathing, but remains unconscious]* Assess the quality and rate of breathing by placing a hand on the casualty's chest. Check circulation (skin temperature and condition) *[Breathing is effective, skin is cold and clammy]*

[Secondary survey is not required as medical help will arrive soon]

Give first aid for shock, monitor casualty's condition. Continue to check ABCs until medical help takes over. Record the events, with any changes that may occur and report to medical attendants when they arrive

One rescuer CPR–Adult

An adult casualty is lying face up. There are no bystanders. The first aider witnessed the incident. There is a telephone nearby.

Activity

SCENE SURVEY

- take charge of the situation
- call out for help and assess hazards at the scene
- determine the number of casualties, what happened, and the mechanism of injury
- identify yourself and offer to help

- assess responsiveness

- send/call for medical help

PRIMARY SURVEY (ABCs)

- airway
- breathing

- circulation

SECONDARY SURVEY

ONGOING CASUALTY CARE

Performance Guidelines

Approach from within the casualty's line of sight

Make the area safe. To protect yourself, put on latex or vinyl gloves if available

You witnessed the collapse and you do not suspect head or spinal injuries

Identify yourself and ask for consent. If the casualty doesn't respond, you have implied consent

Ask, "Are you O.K.?" and gently tap the casualty's shoulders *[Casualty does not respond]*

Give the following information: what happened, location, and that the casualty is unresponsive

A Open the airway using the head-tilt, chin-lift

B Look, listen and feel for up to 10 seconds to check for breathing *[Casualty is not breathing]* Give two slow breaths (2 seconds each) watching the chest to make sure it rises and falls *[The chest rises and falls]*

C Check for signs of circulation (pulse, movement, coughing, etc.) for no more than 10 seconds
[There are no signs of circulation]

Locate the bottom edge of the rib cage, and landmark for chest compressions
Keep arms straight, elbows locked in posiiton and shoulders positioned directly above the heel of the hands so that each compression is straight down on the breastbone

Give cycles of 15 compressions and 2 slow ventilations for about one minute. Use any memory to maintain the correct rate of 100 compressions per minute, e.g.:

　　　　1 and 2 and 3 and 4 and 5 and

　　　　1 and 2 and 3 and 4 and 10 and

　　　　1 and 2 and 3 and 4 and 15

Recheck for signs of circulation for no more than 10 seconds, after one minute and every few minutes after that *[There is still no breathing or pulse]*

Continue CPR until the pulse is restored, until medical help takes over, until another first aider trained in CPR takes over or until you are physically exhausted and unable to continue *[The casualty is not breathing and has no pulse]*

In this situation the first aider continues CPR until medical help arrives. The first aider has not progressed from the primary survey *before help arrives*

Two rescuer CPR–Adult

An adult casualty is lying face up. There is a bystander present.

Activity

First aiders are positioned on opposite sides of the casualty

SCENE SURVEY

- start scene survey

PRIMARY SURVEY (ABCs)

- airway
- breathing

- circulation

Perform cycles of 15 compressions and 2 ventilations for about **one minute** (4 cycles)

Continue CPR for a few minutes and then proceed with a **Switch-over**

SEC.SURVEY/ONGOING CARE
The first aiders continue CPR until medical help takes over

Performance Guidelines

1st rescuer

Start in the role of ventilator

Take charge, call out for help, assess hazards, make area safe, determine what happened, identify yourself and offer to help

Assess responsiveness[Casualty does not respond]

Send the bystander for medical help

Open the airway

Check for breathing [Casualty is not breathing] Give 2 slow ventilations. [The chest rises and falls with each ventilation]

Check for signs and circulation for no more than 10 seconds [There are no signs of circulation]

Give two slow ventilations after each set of 15 compressions and then monitor compressions

After one minute, say "Stop compressions" Complete the cycle with two ventilations and check for signs of circulation [There are still no signs of circulation]. Say " Resume compressions"

Check for signs of circulation every few minutes, after the ventilation cycle.
Give 2 slow ventilations then move to the chest and landmark to take new role as compressor

Resume compressions

2nd rescuer

Start in the role of compressor

Assist with scene survey if needed

Stand by

Landmark for correct hand position.

Give 15 compressions—Use a memory aid to achieve the correct rate of 100 compressions per minute, e.g.: 1 and 2 and 3 and 4 and keeping hands in position to allow for two slow ventilations from the ventilator

Pause, keeping hands in position

Continue with cycles of 15 compressions

After a set of 15 compressions, say **"Switch"**

Move into position beside the head and prepare to check for signs of circulation, take the role of ventilator

Confirm no circulation and say, "Resume compressions"

Artificial respiration—Child

A child casualty is lying face down. The first aider witnessed the incident. A guardian is present.

Activity	Performance Guidelines

SCENE SURVEY

- take charge of the situation

  Approach from within the casualty's line of sight

- call out for help and assess hazards

  Ask the parent or guardian to standby. Make the area safe. To protect yourself, put on latex or vinyl gloves if available

- determine the number of casualties, what happened, and the mechanism of injury

  Question the guardian to determine what happened and the mechanism of injury *[Head/spinal injuries are not suspected]*

- identify yourself and offer to help

  Identify yourself and ask for consent from the guardian

- assess responsiveness

  Ask, "Are you O.K.?" and gently tap the child's shoulders *[Child does not respond]*

- send for medical help

  Give the following information: what happened, location, and that the child is unresponsive

PRIMARY SURVEY (ABCs)

Turn the child onto his back

- airway

  A Open the airway using the head-tilt chin-lift

- breathing

  B Look, listen and feel for up to 10 seconds to check for breathing *[Casualty is not breathing]* Give two slow breaths (**1 to 1.5 seconds each**) using just enough air to make the chest rise and fall with each breath. *[The chest rises and falls]*

- circulation

  C Check for signs of circulation for no more than 10 seconds *[There are signs of circulation]*

  Continue ventilations. One slow breath every 3 seconds for about one minute

Complete the primary survey

  Maintain head tilt and recheck for signs of circulation for no more than 10 seconds after one minute (and every few minutes thereafter*)* *[The child is now breathing.]*

check breathing

  Check the rate, thythm and quality of breathing *[Breathing is effective]*

check circulation

  Check for shock (skin condition and temperature) and do a rapid body survey *[Casualty is in shock but is not bleeding]*

SECONDARY SURVEY
ONGOING CASUALTY CARE

  [Secondary survey is not required as medical help will arrive soon]

- give first aid for shock

  Place the child into the recovery position. Cover, and loosen clothing. Do not give anything by mouth

- monitor casualty's condition and record the events

  Reassess ABCs often. Take notes of the child's condition and any changes that may occur

- report on what happened

  Present an oral report to medical attendants

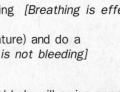

Choking–Child conscious becoming unconscious

A child is grasping at his throat and coughing forcefully. A parent or guardian is present.

Activity

Performance Guidelines

SCENE SURVEY

- take charge of the situation

Approach from within the casualty's line of sight

- call out for help and assess hazards at the scene

Ask the guardian to stand by. Make the area safe. To protect yourself, put on latex or vinyl gloves if available

- determine the number of casualties, what happened, and the mechanism of injury

Ask "Are you choking?" [The casualty is coughing forcefully]

- identify yourself and offer to help

Identify yourself and ask for consent from the parent or guardian

PRIMARY SURVEY (ABCs)

- airway

A   Do not intervene at this time—encourage coughing
Watch for signs of complete obstruction

[The child now cannot cough, breathe or speak]
When coughing stops, ask "Can you cough?"
Stand or kneel behind the child and landmark—give inward and upward abdominal thrusts until the airway is cleared or the child becomes unconscious

[The child becomes unconscious]
Ease the child to the floor on his back

- send for medical help

Give the following information: what happened, location, number of casualties and that the child is choking and unconscious

Look in the mouth [Nothing is visible]

Open the airway and check for breathing [No breathing]

Try to ventilate [Chest does not rise]

Reposition the head, check the seals and try to ventilate again [Chest still does not rise]

Landmark - Give 5 chest compressions, keeping the airway open with the other hand, then look in the mouth again [The object is seen and removed]

- breathing

B   Give 1 slow breath (1-1.5 seconds) checking that the chest rises and falls [Chest rises and falls] Give a second breath, watching the chest rise and fall

- circulation

    Complete primary survey

C   Check for signs of circulation for no more than 10 seconds [The child is breathing but remains unconscious] Assess the quality and rate of breathing by placing a hand on the child's chest. Check circulation (skin temperature and condition) [Breathing is effective, skin is cold and clammy]

SECONDARY SURVEY

[Secondary survey is not required as medical help will arrive soon]

ONGOING CASUALTY CARE

Turn into the recovery position and give first aid for shock. Continue to check ABCs until medical help takes over. Record the events along with any changes that may occur and report to medical attendants when they arrive

One rescuer CPR–Child

An unconscious child casualty is lying face up. A parent or guardian who witnessed the incident is present.

Activity

SCENE SURVEY

- take charge of the situation

- call out for help and assess hazards at the scene

- determine the number of casualties, what happened, and the mechanism of injury

- identify yourself and offer to help

- assess responsiveness

- send for medical help

PRIMARY SURVEY (ABCs)

- airway

- breathing

- circulation

Performance Guidelines

Approach from within the casualty's line of sight

Make the area safe. To protect yourself, put on latex or vinyl gloves if available

Question the parent or guardian to determine what happened and the mechanism of injury. *[Head/spinal injuries are not suspected]*

Identify yourself and ask for consent from the parent or guardian

Ask, "Are you O.K.?" and gently tap the child's shoulders *[Child does not respond]*

Give the following information: what happened, location, and that the child is unresponsive

A   Open the airway using the head-tilt, chin-lift

B   Look, listen and feel for up to 10 seconds to check for breathing. *[Child is not breathing]*. Give two slow breaths (1 to 1.5 seconds each) watching the chest to make sure it rises and falls *[The chest rises and falls]*

C   Check for signs of circulation for no more than 10 seconds *[There is no pulse]*

Locate the bottom edge of the rib cage, and landmark to find the lower part of the breastbone. Give 5 chest compressions with the heel of one hand. Keep arm straight, elbow locked in position and shoulders positioned directly above the heel of the hands so that each compression is straight down on the breastbone. Keep the airway open with the other hand.

Give cycles of 5 compressions and 1 slow ventilation for about one minute. Use any memory aid to maintain the correct rate of 100 compressions per minute, e.g.:

   1, 2, 3, 4, 5

Recheck for signs of circulation for no more than 10 seconds, after one minute and every few minutes after that *[There are still no signs of circulation]*

Continue CPR until circulation is restored, until medical help takes over, until another first aider trained in CPR takes over or until you are physically exhausted and unable to continue *[The child is not breathing and has no pulse]*

SECONDARY SURVEY

ONGOING CASUALTY CARE

In this situation the first aider continues CPR until medical help arrives. The first aider has not progressed from the primary survey before help arrives

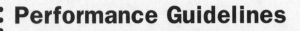
Artificial respiration—Infant

An infant casualty is lying face up. A parent or guardian who witnessed the incident is present.

Activity	**Performance Guidelines**

SCENE SURVEY

- take charge of the situation

  Approach from within the casuatly's line of sight

- call out for help and assess hazards at the scene

  Make the area safe. To protect yourself, put on latex or vinyl gloves if available

- determine the number of casualties, what happened, and the mechanism of injury

  Question the parent or guardian to determine what happened and the mechanism of injury. *[Head/spinal injuries are not suspected]*

- identify yourself and offer to help

  Identify yourself and ask for consent from the parent or guardian

- assess responsiveness

  Gently tap the bottom of the infant's feet *[Infant does not respond]*

- send for medical help

  Give the following information: what happened, location, and that the infant is unresponsive

PRIMARY SURVEY (ABCs)

- airway

  A   Open the airway using the head-tilt chin-lift
       Do not over extend the neck

- breathing

  B   Look, listen and feel for up to 10 seconds to check for breathing *[Infant is not breathing]* Make a good seal over the infant's mouth and nose. Give two slow, breaths using just enough air to make the chest rise. Check to see if the chest rises and falls with each breath.
       [The chest rises and falls]

- circulation

  C   Check for signs of circulation (a brachial pulse, movement, coughing, etc.) for no more than 10 seconds. *[There are signs of circulation]*

Continue ventilations

Give one slow breath every three seconds for about one minute

Recheck for signs of circulation after one minute (and every few minutes thereafter)

Maintain head tilt. Recheck for signs of circulation for no more than 10 seconds

Continue ventilations until the breathing is restored, until medical help takes over, until another first aider takes over or until you are physically exhausted and unable to continue
[The infant is not breathing, but has other signs of circulation]

SECONDARY SURVEY

ONGOING CASUALTY CARE

In this situation the first aider continues AR until medical help arrives. The first aider has not progressed from the primary survey before help arrives

Choking–Infant conscious becoming unconscious

An infant appears to be struggling and coughing forcefully. A parent or guardian who witnessed the incident is present.

Activity

SCENE SURVEY

- take charge of the situation
- call out for help and assess hazards at the scene
- determine the number of casualties, what happened, and the mechanism of injury
- identify yourself and offer to help

PRIMARY SURVEY (ABCs)

- airway

- send for medical help

- breathing

- circulation
  Complete the primary survey

SECONDARY SURVEY

ONGOING CASUALTY CARE

Performance Guidelines

Approach from within the casualty's line of sight

To protect yourself, put on latex or vinyl gloves if available

Question the parent or guardian to determine what happened and the mechanism of injury. [Head/spinal injuries are not suspected]

Identify yourself and ask for consent from the parent or guardian

A   Identify the degree of obstruction

[The infant is blue in the face and gagging].
Position the infant face down with the head lower than the trunk. Give 5 back blows between the shoulder blades then turn the infant. Give 5 chest thrusts with two fingers one finger's width below the nipple line

Repeat back blows and chest thrusts until the obstruction is removed or the infant becomes unconscious
[The infant becomes unconscious]

Give the following information: what happened, location, and that the infant is unresponsive

Look in the mouth *[Nothing is visible]*

Open the airway and check for breathing *[No breathing]*

Try to ventilate. *[Chest does not rise]*. Reposition the head, check the seals and try to ventilate again. *[Chest still does not rise]*

Begin CPR- Give 5 chest compressions. Repeat foreign body checks, attempts to ventilate, and chest compressions until the airway is cleared, medical help takes over or you cannot continue. *[The object is seen and removed]*

B   Give 1 slow breath (1-1.5 seconds each) checking that the chest rises and falls. *[Chest rises and falls]*. Give a second breath, watching the chest rise and fall. Check for breathing for up to 10 seconds *[The infant is breathing]*.
Assess the quality of breathing *[Breathing is effective]*.

C   Check for shock. A rapid body survey is not required as other injuries are not suspected. *[The infant is in shock]*

[Secondary survey is not required as medical help will arrive soon]

Give first aid for shock, monitor the infant's condition. Continue to check ABCs until medical help takes over. Record the events along with any changes that may occur and report to medical attendants when they arrive

One rescuer CPR–Infant

An unconscious infant is lying face up. A parent or guardian who witnessed the incident is present.

Activity	Performance Guidelines

Activity

SCENE SURVEY

- take charge of the situation

- call out for help and assess hazards at the scene

- determine the number of casualties, what happened, and the mechanism of injury

- identify yourself and offer to help

- assess responsiveness

- send for medical help

PRIMARY SURVEY (ABCs)

- airway

- breathing

- circulation

SECONDARY SURVEY AND ONGOING CASUALTY CARE

Performance Guidelines

Approach from within the casualty's line of sight

Make the area safe. To protect yourself, put on latex or vinyl gloves if available

Question the parent or guardian to determine what happened and the mechanism of injury. [Head/spinal injuries are not suspected]

Identify yourself and ask for consent from the parent or guardian

Gently tap the bottom of the infant's feet
[Infant does not respond]

Give the following information: what happened, location, and that the infant is unresponsive

A   Open the airway using the head-tilt chin-lift
Do not over extend the neck

B   Look, listen and feel for up to 10 seconds to check for breathing [Infant is not breathing]. Make a good seal over the infant's mouth and nose. Give two slow breaths using just enough air to make the chest rise. Check to see if the chest rises and falls with each breath. [The chest rises and falls]

C   Check for signs of circulation for no more than 10 seconds [There are no signs of circulation]

Landmark to find the lower part of the breastbone and give 5 compressions with two fingers, one finger width below the nipple line.

Use any memory aid to maintain the correct rate of at least 100 compressions per minute e.g.:
        1, 2, 3, 4, 5

Give cycles of 5 compressions and 1 slow ventilation for about one minute

Recheck for signs of circulation for no more than 10 seconds, after one minute and every few minutes after that. [There are still no signs of circulation]

Continue CPR until circulation is restored, until medical help takes over, until another first aider trained in CPR takes over or until you are physically exhausted and unable to continue. [The infant has no signs of circulation]

In this situation the first aider continues CPR until medical help arrives. The first aider has not progressed from the primary survey before help arrives

AED SCENARIO 1 (Two Rescuers- Shockable Rhythm .)

You are in your working area when you receive a call for help from another department. You grab an AED a with a second rescuer you proceed to the scene. When you arrive you notice one of the managers is lying the ground face down and he appears to be unconscious. You start your assessment.

Activity

Performance Guidelines

SCENE SURVEY

Take charge

Make the area safe

Identify yourself and ask for consent

Ask, "Are you O.K.?" and gently tap the casualty's shoulders
[Casualty does not respond]

Send/call for medical help. Tell them what happened, location and that the casualty is unresponsive

PRIMARY SURVEY (ABCs)

A   Open the airway

B   Check breathing for no more than 10 seconds
[Casualty is not breathing]

Give two slow breaths (2 seconds each) watching the chest
[The chest rises and falls]

C   Check for signs of circulation for no more than 10 seconds
[There are no signs of circulation]

Second rescuer:

Landmark for chest compressions

Give cycles of 15 compressions and 2 slow ventilations until AED is ready t be attached.

DEFIBRILLATION

First rescuer:

Turn machine on. Listen for voice prompts.

Attach cable to AED

Attach electrode pads

Attach pads to chest

Clear casualty-Press analyze

Shock indicated

Clear casualty-Shock

Analyze and shock 2 more times

Check circulation, if none - CPR for 1 minute

Clear- analyze and shock 3 times as indicated by the AED

Check pulse-if no pulse CPR for 1 minute

Continue sequence till medical help arrives

AED SCENARIO 2 (Two Rescuers- Non Shockable Rhythm)

You are providing first aid services at a hockey game. A person comes rushing up to you telling you that someone has collapsed in the stands. You grab an AED and with a second rescuer you proceed to the scene. You start your assessment.

Activity

Performance Guidelines

SCENE SURVEY

Take charge

Make the area safe

Identify yourself and ask for consent

Ask, "Are you O.K.?" and gently tap the casualty's shoulders
[Casualty does not respond]

Send/call for medical help. Tell them what happened, location and that the casualty is unresponsive

PRIMARY SURVEY (ABCs)

A   Open the airway

B   Check breathing for no more than 10 seconds
[Casualty is not breathing]

Give two slow breaths (2 seconds each) watching the chest
[The chest rises and falls]

C   Check for signs of circulation for no more than 10 seconds
[There are no signs of circulation]

Second rescuer:

Landmark for chest compressions

Give cycles of 15 compressions and 2 slow ventilations until AED is ready to be attached.

DEFIBRILLATION

First rescuer:

Turn machine on. Listen for voice prompts.

Attach cable to AED

Attach electrode pads

Attach pads to chest

Clear casualty—Press analyze

Machine says "No shock indicated" "Check pulse."

Check for signs of circulation—if none—CPR for 1 minute

Clear casualty—Press analyze

Machine says "No shock indicated" "Check pulse."

Check for signs of circulation—if none—CPR for 1 minute

Clear casualty—Press analyze

Machine says "No shock indicated" "Check pulse."

Check for signs of circulation—if none—CPR for 1 minute

Continue CPR until medical help takes over.

AED SCENARIO 3 (Lone Rescuer- Shockable Rhythm)

You are working with your partner who suddenly falls to the ground. You grab an AED and call out for help. Nobody answers your call for assistance. You start your assessment.

Activity	Performance Guidelines
SCENE SURVEY	Take charge
	Make the area safe
	Identify yourself and ask for consent
	Ask, "Are you O.K.?" and gently tap the casualty's shoulders *[Casualty does not respond]*
	Send/call for medical help. Tell them what happened, location and that the casualty is unresponsive
PRIMARY SURVEY (ABCs)	A Open the airway
	B Check breathing for no more than 10 seconds *[Casualty is not breathing]*
	Give two slow breaths (2 seconds each) watching the chest *[The chest rises and falls]*
	C Check for signs of circulation for no more than 10 seconds *[There are no signs of circulation]*
DEFIBRILLATION	Turn machine on. Listen for voice prompts.
	Attach cable to AED
	Attach electrode pads
	Attach pads to chest
	Clear casualty-Press analyze
	Shock indicated
	Clear casualty-Shock
	Analyze and shock 2 more times (if shock indicated)
	Check for signs of circulation, if none—CPR for 1 minute
	Clear- analyze and shock 3 times (if shock indicated)
	Check for signs of circulation, if none—CPR for 1 minute
	Clear- analyze and shock 3 times (if shock indicated)
	Check for signs of circulation, if none—CPR for 1 minute
	Continue sequence till medical help arrives

Answers to the instructor-led exercises

For your reference, the answers to the instructor-led exercises throughout the activity book are given below:

Instructor-led Exercise 4

A1 can
A2 forceful
A3 wheezing
A4 reddish
A5 encourage coughing

B1 cannot
B2 ineffective
B3 high-pitched noises
B4 bluish
B5 first aid

C1 cannot
C2 impossible
C3 no sound; cannot
C4 bluish
C5 first aid

Instructor-led Exercise 8

1. blood pressure
2. constantly
3a. thick and less elastic
3b. enlarged
4. almost never
5. fatty deposits
6. b
7. coronary artery disease
8. a, b, c, d, f
9. oxygen
10. narrowed
11. blood clot; heart muscle
12. oxygen
13. angina
14. pumping blood
15. sudden death
16. (in any order)
    heart attack
    trauma/injuries
    stroke
    electrical shock
    poisoning
    stopped breathing
17. oxygen
18. blockage; brain
19. stroke

WHAT NEXT?!

Congratulations!

You have successfully completed a St. John Ambulance First Aid course. What next? Why not put your new skills to use, and become a volunteer member of St. John Ambulance.

Join the Brigade

▶ **serve your community**—provide first aid services at local events, and take part in other programmes such as hospital or school visits.

▶ **learn more first aid, CPR and patient care skills (free of charge)**—ongoing training for Brigade members integrates first aid, CPR and patient care skills along with practical and written assessments.

▶ **develop leadership skills**—take advantage of leadership training and apply it in leadership positions at all levels of the Brigade.

▶ **make new friends**—there are approximately 500 Brigade divisions across the country, made up of over 11,000 people, like yourself, who want to share their time and skills with their communities.

▶ **earn recognition**—your involvement in the Brigade will be appreciated by employers and schools. Your achievements will be recognized through our extensive awards programme.

Become an Instructor

▶ **teach courses to the public**—further your knowledge and techniques through the National Instructor Training and Development Programme, and share your talents through community-based courses.

▶ **earn an honorarium**—expenses incurred by you in implementing courses will be covered by an honorarium.

▶ **help Canadians to help themselves**—with your help, Canadians will learn new skills in the variety of courses offered by St. John Ambulance.

▶ **gain experience speaking in front of a group**—you will have an opportunity to speak to Canadians young and old, and from a variety of cultural backgrounds. Each new group offers new and different challenges.

▶ **develop lasting friendships**—participating as a St. John instructor will have a positive effect on you not only from fellow instructors but also from your students.

Share your skills—join the St. John family.
For more information, contact your local Branch of St. John Ambulance today!

St. John Ambulance

FIRST AID EXAMINATION ANSWER SHEET
Emergency and Standard Levels

PLEASE PRINT

Student's Name: _____ Date: _____

Provincial Council/Special Centre: _____

Final marks: Section 1: ____/20 *(Pass = 14/20)* Section 2: ____ / ____

1–5 Compulsory Lessons ✔

1. a b c d
2. a b c d
3. a b c d
4. a b c d
5. a b c d
6. a b c d
7. a b c d
8. a b c d
9. a b c d
10. a b c d
11. a b c d
12. a b c d
13. a b c d
14. a b c d
15. a b c d
16. a b c d
17. a b c d
18. a b c d
19. a b c d
20. a b c d

6 Child Resuscitation

21. a b c d
22. a b c d
23. a b c d
24. a b c d

7 Infant Resuscitation

25. a b c d
26. a b c d
27. a b c d

28. a b c d
29. a b c d
30. a b c d

8 Cardiovascular Emergencies/CPR

31. a b c d
32. a b c d
33. a b c d
34. a b c d
35. a b c d
36. a b c d

9 Two-rescuer CPR

37. a b c d
38. a b c d

10 Secondary Survey

39. a b c d
40. a b c d
41. a b c d
42. a b c d

11 Bone and Joint Injuries—Upper Limbs; Muscle Strains

43. a b c d
44. a b c d
45. a b c d
46. a b c d

12 Bone and Joint Injuries—Lower Limbs

47. a b c d
48. a b c d
49. a b c d

50. a b c d
51. a b c d
52. a b c d

13 Head/Spinal and Pelvic Injuries

53. a b c d
54. a b c d

14 Chest Injuries

55. a b c d
56. a b c d
57. a b c d
58. a b c d

15 Wound Care

59. a b c d
60. a b c d
61. a b c d
62. a b c d

16 Multiple Casualty Management

63. a b c d
64. a b c d
65. a b c d
66. a b c d

17 Rescue Carries

67. a b c d
68. a b c d

18 Eye Injuries

69. a b c d
70. a b c d

19 Burns

71. a b c d
72. a b c d

20 Poisons, Bites and Stings

73. a b c d
74. a b c d

21 Medical Conditions

75. a b c d
76. a b c d

22 Environmental Illnesses and Injuries

77. a b c d
78. a b c d

23 Emergency Childbirth and Miscarriage

79. a b c d
80. a b c d

24 Automated External Defibrillation

81. a b c d
82. a b c d
83. a b c d
84. a b c d
85. a b c d
86. a b c d
87. a b c d
88. a b c d
89. a b c d
90. a b c d